The Inspired Journey

A Woman's Blueprint for Spirit-Filled Living

by

Sandye Brown and Alexis Mason

authorHOUSE™

1663 LIBERTY DRIVE, SUITE 200
BLOOMINGTON, INDIANA 47403
(800) 839-8640
WWW.AUTHORHOUSE.COM

First published by AuthorHouse 05/24/05

ISBN: 1-4208-3620-X (sc)

Library of Congress Control Number: 2005902005

Printed in the United States of America
Bloomington, Indiana

This book is printed on acid-free paper.

Table of Contents

Acknowledgments

One of the richest blessings brought to us as we go to publication of this book is the opportunity to thank the many people who have enthusiastically encouraged us to continue our work. Without them, this book would have remained a dream on the "someday" list.

To our husbands, Ben Carr and Dave Mason: You have loved us, encouraged us, and reminded us that we have something to offer.

To the women who have attended our workshops: Thank you for telling us how we have changed your perspective loudly enough for us to hear you.

To our personal mentors: You have given us the keys to step out in faith and to prove to ourselves that the blueprint works.

To our friends and colleagues who read our manuscript and gave us much valuable input and direction: Tasha Angel, Charlie Cabrera, Mary Closson, Beth Forsythe, Ruth Mathis, Dave Mason, Becky Munson, Joy Overstreet, Lynne Perry, Nancy Pionk, and Shelly Turner. Thank you, thank you, for the generous contribution of your time and expertise, for sharing your impressions with us and for helping the book to evolve and grow.

Preface

Don't just read this book. It has been designed to be an interactive experience. The benefits you receive will be in direct proportion to the responses you record in each of the exercises. You may want to read through an entire chapter first and then go back and work through the suggested exercises. Use the exercises to stimulate your own reflections, your own age-old wisdom, your own connection to the spiritual, and so on. The rewards will come from your honesty, your willingness to examine the issues addressed in each chapter, and your written record of your place along the journey. It's not what we say that counts; it's what you do with what we say that counts.

Pick up the book, open it anywhere, work through the elements of the chapter, put it down, pick it up again. You will discover that each time you consider the main theme of each chapter you will bring a different "you" to the experience. Allow your subconscious to ponder the questions and exercises that may be a struggle the first time you address them. The second time, the third time, and so on will reveal much more to you.

Our prayer for you as you explore, affirm and challenge yourself, and grow in self-awareness is that you allow the potential within you to lead you to the abundant blessings that are your birthright.

This book is intended to help you establish a stronger spiritual foundation wherein you become more self-aware and more empowered in your life. The basis of this foundation consists of:

- Making more conscious and life-affirming choices
- Listening to and heeding the voice of Spirit
- Surrendering areas of struggle
- Actively cultivating your relationship with Spirit to help you tap into your God-given greatness

Your new awareness, shaped by a stronger connection with God, will help you to reinvent yourself by replacing old habits, reaffirming your blessings, and ultimately allowing you to affirm your greatness and use it to serve others.

Each chapter follows the same pattern.

PERSONAL REFLECTION
Intended to introduce the theme by using our own experiences, stories about ourselves, and stories about our families, this section is designed to encourage you to think about your own story in relation to the topic.

LOOKING INWARD
This section is an opportunity to explore several levels of meaning related to the theme of the chapter. We use this opportunity to "teach" to the concepts, providing examples, illustrations, charts, and other materials to bring the information to life.

WISDOM FROM THE AGES
Both of us have always loved stories. Listening to stories as children, discovering the magic of reading, and "living" the adventures of the main characters we met in books is part of the richness of our heritage. We chose stories from a variety of sources to illustrate the theme for each chapter. We hope that the stories will strike a chord within you as well. You will probably be able to think of additional stories from many lands that lend themselves to the points we are discussing. We encourage you to keep a record of stories that you can draw upon to reinforce the concepts we are sharing with you.

KEY THOUGHTS
This section presented us with another opportunity to teach to the concept. There are also activities embedded in this section for which you may wish to do some journaling, participate in a discussion group, or upon which you may want to pray or meditate.

CONNECTING TO THE SPIRITUAL
This section continues the opportunity for you to interact with the material and includes some useful prayer suggestions. It also serves as a review of the main points. It is structured to point out or reinforce the relationship we have with The Eternal Spirit and provides an additional opportunity to record your thoughts.

PERSONAL MEDITATION
This section speaks to the power of affirmations, those statements that empower and encourage us. The use of visualization and

relaxation techniques are included to help you focus and train your mind to relax, to be receptive, and to maintain a positive mind set.

SERVING OTHERS

The exercises and information in this section teach you how to be available to others as you increase your own sense of self worth. An increased sense of self worth will enhance your ability to apply the skills you are learning and help you become the best person you can be based upon your own highest standards.

PUTTING IT ALL TOGETHER

This section is the call to action that will help you apply the concepts and themes to your own patterns of behavior. You will be challenged to take a stand, to identify changes you need to make, and to make plans to implement those changes.

Taken as a whole, this book will provide you with strategies that you can use right now to make a difference in your life and to make a significant contribution to the lives of those around you. It is worthy work. You are worthy of the effort and satisfaction that you will realize.

Above all, enjoy the process; enjoy the journey; challenge yourself to grow as you work. Share the experience with another if you wish and celebrate the uniqueness of each person's journey. Your life is a gift from God. What you do with it is your gift to everyone around you and ultimately to God.

"The Blueprint"

| Reinventing Yourself | Replacing Old Habits | Reaffirming Your Blessings |

← ————— **Tapping Into Your Greatness** ————— →

Spirit

← ————— **Establishing a Strong Foundation** ————— →

| Empowered To Choose | Empowered To Listen | Empowered To Surrender | Empowered To Awaken |

The Blueprint for Spirit-Filled Living entails establishing a strong foundation that empowers you to: make more proactive choices, listen more deeply for the urgings of Spirit, cultivate a surrendered approach to life, and become more awake to the workings of Spirit in your life.

These foundational skills cultivate a relationship to Spirit that allows you to tap into your God-given greatness.

Your new awareness will assist you to reinvent yourself by replacing old habits, reaffirming your blessings, and ultimately allowing you to claim your greatness and use it to serve others.

Introduction

Unleash Your Greatest Power

The Story of Sir Gawain and Dame Ragnell

One day King Arthur went hunting in the forest of Inglewood with his retainers. At length he and his companions became separated and he found himself in an unfamiliar part of the forest.

Abruptly, he found that his body was quite frozen and he could not move a muscle. A menacing figure, dressed in pitch-black armor approached him, saying, "Arthur, I have you in my power. You have wrongfully given my lands to Sir Gawain and for that, you will die unless you find the answer to a question I put to you."

Arthur found that he could speak and asked, "Who are you, and what is this question you wish me to answer?"

"I am The Black Knight. If you would win your life, return here in a year with an answer to this question: *What is it that every woman desires most?* " As suddenly as he had appeared, he was gone and the King found that he could move freely again. He returned to his court with a heavy heart.

Of all his retainers, only Sir Gawain asked King Arthur what sorrow he bore, and Arthur related the tale of his discomfiture in the forest. Sir Gawain then proposed that they ride forth and ask every woman they found what she most desires and collect the answers in a book.

They set out and asked women what they desired and soon they had a huge book of answers. But as many as they had found, they were still uneasy that any of the answers they had was the true one.

Shortly before the King had to meet with The Black Knight, he rode again through the forest of Inglewood and came upon a hideously ugly woman, one whose ugliness was so great that original texts go on for many a verse describing it. She stopped him saying that she had the right answer and could save his life, if he agreed to her terms. He asked what these were, and she replied, "I am Dame Ragnell and I want to marry one of your knights, Sir Gawain."

King Arthur was horrified, and told her that he could not promise her Gawain without his consent and that he would return to her after speaking with Gawain. He returned to court and explained the situation to Gawain. Without hesitation, Gawain answered that he would marry her in a minute, even if she was a devil, if it would help Arthur.

Arthur returned to the forest where Dame Ragnell was waiting. He told her that Gawain had agreed to marry her if her answer was the one sought, but if one of the others they had collected was the one, the deal was off. Satisfied with this, she gave Arthur the answer.

On the appointed day, Arthur rode to meet with The Black Knight who again appeared suddenly, demanding the answer to his question. Arthur gave him the book with the answers they collected. The Black Knight looked it over, laughed, and told Arthur to prepare to die. Arthur said, "Wait, I have one more answer," and gave him that of Dame Ragnell.

The Black Knight roared in frustration! "Only my sister could have told you that! May she be burned in the fires of hell for her treachery! Go where you will, King Arthur, I will bother you no more." So, Arthur returned to Ragnell and brought her back with him to court.

Upon seeing her for the first time, Gawain looked stunned, but bravely assented to be married the next day. The ladies of the court wept to see such a kind and handsome knight to be married to such a hideous woman; the knights were glad it wasn't any of them who had to marry her.

Ragnell demanded to be married publicly and to have a great feast with all the nobles attending. She was decked out in the most costly array, but her manners repulsed everyone there. Great was the pity felt for Gawain that day!

At last, it was over and the couple was led to their chamber. There, Gawain gazed at the fire, reluctant to touch his bride, until she requested a kiss. Bravely, he acceded, only to find a most radiant woman in his arms. He stared speechless in wonder and, finally finding his tongue, asked her how could this be.

"I have waited in that shape until I found a man gentle enough to marry me. Now I offer you a choice: I can be fair by night and foul by day; or foul by night and fair by day. Decide which you want."

Gawain thought for a while, pondering the events that had lead to this moment, and then it dawned on him what answer he must give. "I cannot make such a choice; that is for you to decide."

She cried out in joy, "My lord, you are as wise as you are noble and true, for you have given me what every woman genuinely desires - *to be able to be in charge of her own life.* You will never see that hideous old hag again, for I choose to be fair from this time forward."

✳ ✳ ✳ ✳ ✳ ✳ ✳

Some time ago our local Public Broadcasting station aired a program called *Frontier House.* This program was a fascinating study of the contrast between life in the 21st century and life in the 1800's. For the experiment, three families were uprooted from their lives in 2002, trained briefly on how to survive life in the 1800's, stripped of all modern conveniences – which were replaced by the tools and implements of the earlier century – and then transplanted to Montana for five months, armed with what they had learned. Their charge – to homestead a plot of land that could conceivably allow them to survive for five years, after which time the land would be theirs.

Each of the families underwent a radical transformation in the process of settling into the inevitability and enormity of the adjustments they all had to make to deal with the immediate future that stretched ominously before them. Upon their re-entry to our current era, each family spoke about feeling displaced, out of sync with the world they had known and had been so attached to prior to the experiment. They all described it differently, but three themes emerged:

1. A sense of feeling overwhelmed by the sensation of life coming "at" them

2. A feeling of "too muchness" – too much noise, too much bright lighting, too many choices

3. A sense of feeling disconnected and isolated from their truest, most heartfelt priorities

These feelings all describe the view that life is beyond our control and ability to manage it, and the unintentional by-product of being swept along against our will. Yielding to the constant demands on us to BE more, DO more, and HAVE more, we have gotten caught up in an epidemic of "busyness" that presents us with excessive demands on our time and too many choices to make. In our haste, we become unwitting victims of our own choices and find ourselves imprisoned by them while we were looking the other way, so to speak.

However, as the story of Sir Gawain and Dame Ragnell illustrates, the capacity to choose is one of the greatest powers we have available to us as human beings and yet, often, one of our most underused faculties. "Choice" allows us to transform our relationship to our circumstances at any moment.

We don't always experience that we have the power to shape our own lives, even if we know it intellectually. The original version of the story of Sir Gawain and the Dame Ragnell is thought to have been written in the thirteen or fourteenth century and was one of the most popular stories of late medieval England. The story of Sir Gawain and the Dame Ragnell suggests that humankind has long recognized the importance of choice and struggled with how best to realize its power.

Recognizing that we are the composers of our lives requires four distinct and powerful elements:

1. The continuous practice of "being present" in our lives from moment to moment

2. The courage to tell the truth about what's not working in our lives when it's not working

3. The willingness to take the necessary risks to change our attitudes, our habits, our beliefs and ultimately, our lives

4. Opening ourselves to be touched and moved by Spirit

Once you have shifted your relationship to your life situations and experiences, you are able to see new possibilities and options you couldn't see or recognize previously. As you begin to act on the fundamentals of reshaping your life, you will find yourself empowered to reinvent your relationship to the circumstances in your life and supported to "choose" differently. You will find that you are enabled to take the BOLD actions necessary for you to achieve your life as you envision it.

Spirit-filled living is about gaining mastery and competence in successfully living your personal and professional lives in ways that enrich you, bring you peace and connect you to God in more conscious, meaningful and enduring ways. It means creating a life that allows time for reflection, connection and renewal. It means living a life that provides time to revel in, touch, and be touched by that which is most important to you.

We encourage you to take the time to reflect on how you can restore your capacity to choose – to choose to feel, to choose to "exhale", and to choose to connect with what you truly value in your life. And then, start making the choices that allow you to become more inspired in living your life in ways that are special, renewing, and meaningful to you.

Good Journey!!

PART I

ESTABLISHING A STRONG FOUNDATION

Chapter One

Shape Your Own Destiny

PERSONAL REFLECTION

Your Destiny is Your Choice

How do we end up living lives that are not fulfilling? What's required for us to make the kind of choices that help us create more satisfying lives? To explore these questions, I would like to share with you a brief glance at my life and the direction in which I was headed until I realized that I was the only person who could change my life from one that was unfulfilling to one that has been deeply gratifying.

I know that my parents loved me very much but they were often challenged in knowing how best to express that love. They wrestled with their own personal demons while struggling to raise three small children. But their union steadily eroded and eventually crumbled like weathered sandstone by the time I was nine.

The oldest of three children, I was an intellectually gifted child, observant, reflective, constantly questioning and probing for answers about life. I was also extremely sensitive to the inner turmoil of those around me. Sensing my parents' personal struggles, and feeling somehow responsible, as the oldest child, for resolving their problems, I was filled with feelings of powerlessness, fear and anxiety about the stability of life. The sense of deep unease further enveloped my life like a slow moving fog as I attempted to piece together a quality life while working through my own abuse issues.

Not surprisingly, by my mid-twenties, I was a mess! I found myself merely going through the motions of living. Oh, on the surface, I appeared to be leading a successful life: I had attended several great schools; I had married a brilliant young man and I had chosen a potentially lucrative career path. I was also extremely depressed, agoraphobic and alcoholic. I smoked marijuana every day, suffered from a rapidly decaying gall bladder and regularly took the Valium prescribed by my doctor for stress. I was even seeing a therapist because I felt so crazy and suicidal most of the time. I knew I was a mess, but I didn't know what to do about it.

The turning point came for me when, out of desperation, I recognized that somehow I had to make different choices in order to change the inevitable direction of my life and affect a more hopeful outcome.

The second half of my life has been so unlike the first, that I sometimes feel as if there have been two separate people who have lived my existence. When I "woke up," I became conscious of the reality that although I had been victimized in the past, it did not mean that I was a victim in the present. I was certainly not responsible for what had happened to me, but I was responsible for allowing what happened to taint my experience of joy for today and the sense of my own inner power and connection to spirit. Once I saw that I could make different choices about my life, I knew that I could break free from my past to create a life based on my deepest desires.

LOOKING INWARD

There is much we can do to change the quality of our lives. Sometimes the most powerful and profound change we can make is to shift how we perceive those things that limit us. See if you can recognize yourself in the illustration below.

The Electric Fence Syndrome

Little Johnny was visiting his grandfather's farm one summer and as he and his grandfather walked to the pasture one morning, they came to an electric fence. The grandfather looked around carefully and then placed his hand on the fence as he stepped over it. It was obvious to Little Johnny that the power was not turned on and he followed suit.

As they returned from the pasture, Little Johnny asked his grandfather, "Why did you look around before stepping over the wire? For that matter, why have an electric fence at all if you're not going to turn on the power?"

The grandfather smiled and said, "I was just looking to see if any of the cattle were watching me as I approached the fence. Never give them any idea of what they might be able to do. Electric fences don't need to be on all the time. Once cattle learn that they will be shocked, they will graze right up to the fence and stop."

Many of the limitations in our lives are self-imposed. We live life as if the electric fence is fully charged without even noticing that we have kept ourselves imprisoned because we didn't take the simplest risk of all – that of asking ourselves if the limitations we perceive are real or imagined.

- What are the electric fences in your life?

- Where have you allowed people or circumstances to dictate your future possibilities or sense of joy and personal fulfillment?

My electric fences were the difficult experiences and psychological hurdles of childhood. Once I saw that my interpretation of "who I was", based on my past events, was holding me prisoner, I was able to "step over" my electric fences. My life didn't change immediately, but I found myself no longer constrained by the electric fences. The new sense of freedom I gained helped me see new actions I could take to heal myself and truly shape a new destiny for myself.

Shifting my interpretation of the events of my past empowered me, in a very real way, to transmute my pain into power and compassion – for others and for myself. Again, this transformation didn't happen overnight, but it did happen, and today I have become a more resilient human being – a person I respect, admire and love...even with my imperfections.

- What internal changes would you need to shift (attitudes, opinions, beliefs) to begin the process of shaping your destiny?

- What changes would you need to make in your outer circumstances?
  1. What do you need to stop doing?
  2. What do you need to let go of?
  3. What do you need to start doing?

- What specific inner and outer changes are you *willing* to make?

When I was younger, my parents and teachers would say, "Sandye has so much potential," implying, of course, that I wasn't living up to it. To some degree, I think they were right, and for so many years of my life I chased after my elusive potential. Today, thanks to my connection with God and the effort I've put forth to grow and change I feel I am living my purpose.

- Where in your life do you feel you are not living up to your potential?

- What rationalizations or excuses do you make to keep yourself from moving forward?

- What support do you need to help you make more courageous choices on a consistent basis?

WISDOM FROM THE AGES

Hercules Chooses His Path

When Hercules was a few months old, his mother left him asleep in a brave warrior's shield that served as his cradle. While he slept, two venomous snakes crept up on him. Just as the snakes were about to strike, Hercules awoke. With a squeal of delight and without any sign of fear, the little one seized the snakes, one in each hand. Grasping them around the neck, he held on tight. When his mother returned, she was dumbstruck at the sight, but the snakes had been strangled and the infant Hercules was safe. So began the legends of Hercules' conquests over evil.

Hercules, carefully trained in the ways befitting a hero, grew to manhood possessed of marvelous strength and courage. One day while he was still in his youth, Hercules lay down in a valley to sleep through the noonday heat. In his sleep he had a strange dream.

In his dream, Hercules found himself following a path that suddenly split into two, branching off in opposite directions and forcing him to choose which path to take to pursue his journey. One road looked broad and easy and led down to a pleasant city where he saw the gleam of marble palaces amidst green and tempting gardens. The other road was steep and rocky. It was hard to climb and led endlessly upward, growing rockier and rougher at every step till it disappeared into the clouds.

As Hercules stood hesitating and pondering which road to choose, a beautiful maiden came dancing down the smooth and easy roadway. She beckoned him to follow her and called: "Come with me Hercules, down into the pleasant city. There you need not labor all day in the heat of the sun. You can sit continually in the fragrant gardens, listen to the splash of the fountains and the songs of birds, and maidservants will serve you with all you need."

As Hercules looked toward the city, the piping of merry music faintly reached his ears to invite and tempt him still further. Just then, in the second path, a young maiden, quite different from the first, appeared. She wore plain white robes and her eyes were grave, yet sweet, quiet and calm.

"My sister deceives you, Hercules," she said. "The pleasant things offered you down below are not worth having. They are toys and diversions of which you will soon tire and must be bought with a price that will cost you more than you can imagine. Do not descend the mountain to go into the city but climb the mountain path with me. You will find it rough and difficult, it is true. Yet, advancing its heights, you will find the real delights of life of which you can never tire. Moreover, if you have the courage to climb, this road will lead you to your true destiny."

And then in his dream, Hercules turned his back on the first maiden and took the mountain road. By so choosing the mountainous path as his destiny, Hercules forged his life purpose by means of which he devoted his strength to serve the good of humankind.

KEY THOUGHTS

Many of us feel that our lives are somehow controlled by fate and that we have no control over our own destinies. Webster's Dictionary says that

Destiny is the preordained or inevitable course of events considered as something beyond the power or control of man. And,

Fate is the supposed force, principle or power that predetermines events; the inevitable events predestined by this force

Philosophers have always argued whether our futures are open and unfolding or whether they are moving toward some preordained conclusion. Let's just consider that we have more freedom and power to determine our own lives than we may believe, despite what our current circumstances may indicate. This inner capacity is nurtured by living an awakened and conscious existence wherein we begin to intentionally choose our actions. If you examine your life closely, you can see that who you are today is a direct result of the choices you made in the past.

Some of you will argue, as I once did, that you are more a product of what has happened to you in your past than of the choices you have made. Certainly we are born and raised with many factors beyond our control – our genes, family of origin, socioeconomic level, etc. These factors create an invisible and unconscious set of assumptions, values and practices that help shape how we make future choices and decisions. Most of our unconscious choices arise from our instinctual drive to survive, from the desire to do what we think we **should** do, from the attempt to actualize the fantasy life we see in our mind's eye, etc.

Every choice we make, whether conscious or unconscious, affects all the circumstances that follow it. But it is most often our unconscious choices that give rise to the sense of feeling unfulfilled or not fully satisfied with life.

Lessons I've Learned About Choosing One's Destiny

1. **You must reach a place of creative dissatisfaction with the way things are or the way you are.**

   One of my favorite quotes by Gandhi says, "As long as you derive inner help and comfort from anything, you should keep it. Only give up a thing when you want some other condition **so much** that the thing no longer has any attraction for you, or when it seems to interfere with that which is most greatly desired."

   Sad to say, many of us don't find the will to change our circumstances or perspective about who we are until we have reached the depths of despair and have nowhere else to go. We either opt out of life and become depressed and resigned, or we find the strength, resolve, and faith to scale the walls of the pit into which we have fallen.

   Creative dissatisfaction is that level of discontent and agitation that empowers us to become more resourceful as we move toward the conditions that we desire and beyond the safe haven of the status quo.

2. You will have to pay a price to have what you want, and you must be willing to pay it.

The price I had to pay to create a fulfilling, vision-driven life came in the form of sacrifices I had to make. I had to sacrifice who I thought I was (based on my past) for whom I was willing to become. In order to make that sacrifice, I had to abandon being comfortable in life. I had to take on more and larger challenges over and over again. Today, I can see that I continue to grow and learn because I keep expanding my comfort zone and my view of myself.

One of the other risks I had to take was the risk of separating myself from the "tribe-mentality" as Wayne Dyer calls it. Separating ourselves from the tribe means that we learn to transcend our past conditioning by awakening to the inner voice that calls to us to become more. This awakening often comes in the form of disquiet about one's life, a sense that something's missing. It is when we recognize and respond to the pull of our inner voice that we reach the critical opportunity to break away from our conditioning. It is at this point that we make choices that feed our soul. The alternative is to continue to live a life that ultimately serves no one.

One of the major illusions that I had to shatter was the illusion of control. There is a natural propensity in the modern day human being to live behind a veil of illusion that helps us feel that we are in control of life's happenings. We don't even realize that we rest with a sense of false safety behind this veil until personal catastrophes happen to us.

Many of us don't make daring choices in our lives because we don't want to risk the possibility that our lives might venture into areas that seem out of our control. We want neat, easy lives that are effortlessly managed, but, if you stop for a moment and really think about it, <u>life is unmanageable</u>. It is only our ignorance that makes us think we can manage it. To have the life you truly desire, you must be willing to risk the safety of being in control and feeling as if you need to know how it's all going to turn out.

The biggest sacrifice I had to make was that of seeing myself as a lone individual in the world. I had to make the choice to create a life in partnership with God. I made the choice to recognize my connection to my inner spirit, to others and to a power much greater than myself. In recognizing myself as a being connected to a powerful source, I chose to surrender my life to a higher purpose. It is that higher purpose that has given me the courage and strength to trust myself and the choices I make.

3. **Some of our choices are more powerful and life transforming than others.**

You can always make the choice to NOT face your inner demons – whatever they may be and for whatever justifiable reason you may have. However, when you choose not to confront the realities of your life and undertake the challenges that are holding you back from feeling fulfilled and whole, or to take the critical actions that can turn your life around, you are unknowingly making the choice to live a marginal life – a life where you feel controlled and victimized by the circumstances and people around you rather than empowered and blessed.

My personal experiences have shown me that there are two classes of choices: *reactive* and *proactive*. Every move we make in our lives involves choosing one thing over another. Fortunately, much of the process of making so many infinite choices everyday is relegated to our subconscious. If that were not so, we would exhaust ourselves just going through the decision-making process. At the same time, however, <u>because</u> so many of our choices are subconscious, we often become lulled into a somnolent state where we unintentionally abdicate our power to choose. It is at these times, when we are "asleep" to our true selves, that we make reactive choices.

Reactive Choices

Living a marginal life is the direct by-product of making reactive choices. Reactive choices arise out of our instinct to survive. We react to what other people think we should do with our lives, to what society tells us and to other voices that dictate how we **should** live our lives.

Reactive choices are the choices we make while we are numb to our deepest desires and to our inner urgings. When we make reactive choices we are operating in a default mode where the choices we make are not well thought out or where we are not conscious of our motivations and desires.

The primary consequence of making reactive choices is that those choices become an extension of the life we think we **should** be living based on ideas we have inherited from others (parents, peers, social or work groups, etc.) or based on our own ego needs. And, for a while, it becomes comfortable to live in this manner because we gain the approval and acceptance of others by doing so.

However, there often comes a time in our lives where the inner stirring of discontent whispers softly but insistently to us and demands that we wake up. I have had clients who find themselves in a job or career that is sapping them of their vitality and joy of living. In their search for a sense of meaning and contribution in their lives, they discover that they have failed to find either in the place where they spend the majority of their lives – at work. They come to realize that the careers they have given their lives over to are not of their own conscious choice.

"What has happened?" They ask.

What has happened to these people is the result of living by default. Many people are struggling with the lives they have created by default and not by conscious choice. Living by default occurs when we make reactive choices – choices that we don't think deeply about, or choices that we make purely to fulfill a sense of duty or obligation.

Or...we simply fail to actively make choices. Failing to make choices is a powerful choice in itself – a passive choice. We fail to make choices to communicate, to ask for what we want from others, to change our living situations, to get help if we need it, to allow ourselves to show our vulnerability by asking for support, etc.

The problem with reactive choices is that they are intrinsically unsatisfying. When we make reactive choices, our awareness, our sense of feeling empowered and our heart are all missing. Reactive choices occur when we are disconnected from Self – that part of us that becomes enlivened or deadened by the choices we make.

Proactive Choices

Making truly proactive choices in our lives – choices that stimulate us and lead us to a place of purpose, fulfillment and contribution – requires that we move out of the world of "survival" and into the world of "possibility," where purpose, passion, and vision exist.

We find ourselves making proactive choices when we begin to ask ourselves deeper questions about our existence and our purpose in this life.

Such questions might be:

- Who am I?
- What is my life to be used for?
- What is important to me?
- What are my values?
- What is God calling me to do with my life?
- What is holding me back?
- How can I contribute my talents to others?
- Etc.

Passion for living is a gift to us from God that serves as a "controller" of sorts. When we experience passion and a sense of purpose to our actions, there is a place within us that resonates with joy and energizes us.

When I realized that I had to make different choices in order to be healed from the debilitating effects of addiction and dysfunctional living, the choices I began to make were conscious, proactive choices.   It was during this time, that I found myself asking, "What does God want me to make of my life? How do I break free from this addiction and make the necessary changes?"

I had a vision of myself as a contributor to humanity and as a person who explored and lived up to the potential that I had been given. Even though I didn't know how to reach that vision, I found myself empowered to see a new possibility for my life – one that I had never seen before.

The need to make proactive choices becomes obvious when we see ourselves on a self-destructive path or recognize that we have reached a place of deep despair regarding the particular circumstances in which we find ourselves. However, we can also make small, not-so-obvious proactive choices to shift our lives, such as learning how to say "no" or speaking up for ourselves.

What is important about proactive choices is that they are conscious, courageous acts that, when exercised, consistently have the power to dramatically alter our lives and the lives of others – for the better.

The following chart shows the contrast between reactive and proactive choices:

Reactive Choices	Proactive Choices
• Unconscious, instinctive	• Conscious, creative
• An extension of the past	• A departure from the past
• Not well thought out	• Intentional
• Course of least resistance (less risk)	• Awareness of and willingness to take risks
• Don't change one's life much	• Provide a clear vision of where one wants to go that gets clearer as one moves toward it
• Most often made in a vacuum	• May require outside support to accomplish
• Living by default	• Living purposefully

Every choice we make sets in motion a series of events that shapes the unfolding future. At the same time, we close down every other possible future.

- Is the future you're moving toward the one you want?

- What are the three most important choices you've made in your life that have contributed to who you are today? Identify each choice as reactive or proactive. Notice the impact each choice has had on your life.

CONNECTING TO THE SPIRITUAL

Every moment a voice
out of this world
calls on our soul
to wake up and rise

this soul of ours
is like a flame
with more smoke than light

blackening our vision
letting no light through

lessen the smoke and
more light brightens your house
the house you dwell in now
and the abode
you'll eventually move to

now my precious soul
how long are you going to
waste yourself
in this wandering journey
can't you hear the voice
can't you use your swifter wings
and answer the call

Jalaluddin Rumi

Making courageous choices in your life is risky from the perspective that you won't know what the outcome will be until after you have made each choice. The most effective solution to mitigate the risks we feel inside ourselves is to establish and maintain a moment-by-moment, conscious connection with God. With God as our partner, fear seems to melt away and is at once replaced with faith, courage and love.

How can you maintain a conscious connection with Spirit? In addition to prayer and meditation, imagine that God stands beside you and walks with you as your silent invisible partner everywhere you go. When you feel trepidation or anxiety, talk to God and silently ask to have the inner obstacle removed. See yourself being enveloped by God's love and allow your inner walls to fall. What you will feel is a melting away of the emotional block of fear and, in its place, a sense of peace that allows you to take the next step and the next, until you find that you have done the thing you feared.

PERSONAL MEDITATION

The Serenity Prayer

God, grant me the serenity to accept the things I
cannot change, the courage to change the things
I can and the wisdom to know the difference.
Reinhold Niebuhr

Often, we fight the things we cannot change and fear changing the
things we can. The power to shape our own destiny is derived from
our capacity to cease resisting the way things are and to discern
in the moment those things that are ours to change. Acceptance
and discernment must then be fueled by willingness – willingness to
listen to the inner urge that is calling us to change and willingness to
act with the courage that comes from faith.

Meditating upon and connecting inwardly with the words of the
Serenity Prayer will help you perceive the world differently and
reveal to you which changes to make and how best to make them.

SERVING OTHERS
How to Be Available

You might be asking yourself, "How can I serve others by choosing
my destiny?" Someone once told me that if each one of us put our
energies into becoming the best person we could become (based
on our highest standards and principles), that the world would
dramatically change for the better. I truly believe that! To that end,
I believe that one of the most powerful ways in which we can serve
others is by being a role model for those around us.

PUTTING IT ALL TOGETHER

A Sioux Story

The Creator gathered all of Creation and said, "I want
to hide something from the humans until they are ready
for it."

The eagle said, "Give it to me, I will take it to the moon." The Creator said, "No. One day they will go there and find it."

The salmon said, "I will bury it on the bottom of the ocean." "No. They will go there too."

The buffalo said, "I will bury it on the Great Plains." The Creator said, "They will cut into the skin of the Earth and find it even there."

Grandmother Mole, who lives in the breast of Mother Earth, and who has no physical eyes but sees with spiritual eyes, said, "Put it inside of them."

And the Creator said, "It is done. It is the realization that they create their own reality."

If you want a rich and satisfying life, you must do something uncomfortable every day that moves you away from the circumstances you don't want and toward the life you envision for yourself. You create your own reality by the choices you make in your life.

1. Notice where you feel dissatisfied in your life, or think of a change you would like to make but have been putting off. List below three uncomfortable changes you are willing to make immediately.

2. Identify the proactive choices you will need to make.

3. Identify the resources (money, training, etc) you will need and the two to three people you will include as part of your support network to help you accomplish those changes.

4. Lastly, make a plan for how you will stay connected with your God as your Silent Partner.

Use the space below to record the changes you want to make.

What I Will Change	Resources I Need	People in My Support Network

Actions I will take to stay consciously connected to my Silent Partner:

_____

_____

_____

_____

_____

Chapter Two

Listen with Your Heart

PERSONAL REFLECTION

One of my favorite treats to myself is the gift of lazily indulging in a cup of coffee at Starbucks and people-watching. One sun streaked day as I sat in a quiet corner of the sidewalk café waiting for a friend, I took particular interest in how people were interacting with each other. All about me people were visiting together in small groups of two or three both inside and outside the café. Each small group was occupied in what appeared to be very engaging conversations. The conversations I observed were animated at times and wistful at other times where one of the partners appeared to be deep in thought ruminating over what the other was saying or, perhaps, listening to some other private conversation in his or her own head.

Watching the dynamic conversations of those around me made me think about the act of listening and generated a few questions in my mind to be considered in this chapter…
- What is listening?
- How does our listening impact our actions and responses?
- Is it possible to listen in ways that direct us and help us transform our lives?

While you may generally think of listening as an act that occurs in conversation with another or others, in this instance we will be exploring how listening works in the relationship you have with yourself.

As a hypersensitive child, I cried a lot due to frustration or because my tender feelings were hurt. Often, in the midst of my crying episodes, I became aware of my ability to watch myself, almost as an outside observer, and listen to the thoughts that resonated in my mind. On some occasions, when I took the time to tune into those thoughts, I could hear myself talking back to those who had hurt me: either rehearsing what I should have said or fantasizing about what I would say to them in the future. On other occasions, I could hear my lamenting, self-pitying cries about the unfairness of life, my stern scolding voice chastising me for getting myself into such a mess or my villainous bad girl voice vowing to make "them" sorry for treating me so badly.

While becoming conscious of my objective "witness" self was an important development in my awakening, at that time I didn't know that I had any other recourse than to ride out the emotional storms until they had passed.

Many years later, I lost a child through miscarriage. Initially and for a few weeks after the doctor told me I had miscarried, I remained calm and philosophical about what had happened. I put on a brave face for my husband and carried on at my job as if nothing had happened. Then, one day after work, I arrived at an empty house and was overtaken by a deep sense of loss, regret and grief. I began crying and sobbing for my lost baby and allowed myself to feel all the feelings I had suppressed about my loss. After a time, my emotional floodgates opened wider and wider until the weight of all the losses in my life up to that point came pouring down on me. In those moments as my sobs became deeper and wilder, I felt completely out of control and concerned for my own safety and sanity. My only solace during that time was the prayer "God help me" which I repeated over and over.

My prayer was answered in a very strange way...

In an instant, I became aware. I found myself once again being the observer – watching myself as I sobbed and listening to the stream of thoughts pouring through my mind. As I listened, I heard myself repeating – over and over and over and over – that this situation was too much to bear, that I was alone in the world and that no one could help me.

Watching myself and watching my thoughts I had a revelation. I saw that the longer and more earnestly I repeated these thoughts the more despondent, desperate and hopeless I felt. This was a life-altering revelation to me!

Armed with the revelation that my repetitive thoughts were responsible for my sense of hopelessness, I was able to reach deep down inside myself past the pain to the truth – the truth that while I had suffered many disappointments, losses and personal tragedies, I was not alone because I was surrounded by the love of family and by God's love.

As I opened myself to love, I found the strength to replace my painful thoughts with the phrase, "Stop! Everything is going to be okay." At some point during the process of repeating my new affirming thought, I was led to a sanctuary of calmness and peace within me. In that sanctuary, I heard "God loves you."

It is within our inner sanctuary that we learn to listen with our hearts. For it is within this sanctuary that we receive and can hear the still, small voice of God.

LOOKING INWARD

Listening is a more complicated process than we generally think it to be because it entails more than simply hearing the words being uttered by another. In the course of human communications, we must also make sense of the words being said in order to formulate our responses to it. The meaning-making nature of listening suggests that it is not a passive phenomenon.

My dictionary provides the following definitions for listening:

(1) the act of applying oneself to hearing something

(2) paying attention or giving heed to something
(3) tuning in and listening to a broadcast

Listening is the process by which we attend to, apply ourselves to or tune into what we hear. It is the way in which we shape our attention. For example, as I sit here and write, the television is also on in the distant background. While I can hear the television, I am not actively listening to it. I am engaged in the act of listening to myself, to my own thoughts. However, from time to time, as I hear the laugh tracks of the sitcom on the tube, I then shift my attention to listen to the television. This is the first important distinction to know about listening. Namely, that our listening is shaped by what we pay attention to.

The second important distinction to understand about listening is that we are always listening to something – even when we are alone. There is a constant inner dialogue that takes place within us. To test this idea out for yourself, stay quiet for a minute or two and tune in to your inner thoughts. This may be difficult for those of you who are unaccustomed to turning your attention inward, but with practice, you can begin to hear the ongoing stream of your internal dialogue.

It is important to be able to hear and become intimate with your internal dialogue because a vital access to your inner strength is how you relate to those interior conversations.

A common misconception that arises in a discussion about self-listening is that we are advocating the replacement of our emotions with logic or mental aloofness, or that we are suggesting that our emotions are bad – quite the contrary. We are asserting that there are times when our lives or our actions are not as we wish them to be and that there are times when we don't feel good about who we are. It is during these times that a shift in how we listen to ourselves becomes a very potent key to our own transformation.

Listening is the phenomenon that enables us to hear and understand what is being said so that we can formulate our response to what we hear. Much emphasis today is placed on the importance of listening in order to create satisfying personal and professional relationships;

yet, it is interesting that we seldom listen to ***ourselves*** with the goal of understanding what we hear in a way that enables us to respond to it <u>effectively</u>. Even though an incessant internal dialogue takes place within us, we are unaware that it is largely responsible for how we feel and the actions that follow as a result of what we feel.

How we listen to ourselves – our relationship with our internal dialogue – is a vital factor in determining how effective we are at creating fulfilling spirit-filled lives. Listening can be characterized in four distinct ways:

1. "Checked Out"
2. Habitual Listening
3. Generative Listening
4. Sacred Listening

Ways to Relate to Internal Dialogue

Automatic	
"Checked Out"	**Habitual Listening**
• Tuned out; oblivious to one's internal voice and one's external surroundings • Unaware of your inner dialogue	• Hearing your inner dialogue but not listening to it • Not questioning the veracity of what you hear or challenging the assumptions you tell yourself

Intentional	
Generative Listening	**Sacred Listening**
• Paying attention to your inner dialogue and how you speak to yourself • Noticing your self-limiting inner dialogue and replacing it with more self-affirming and empowering statements	• Turning inward with an intention to tune into the calmness of one's inner sanctuary • Allowing the still, small voice of God to emerge from beneath all other internal messages • Surrendering one's control to allow God's power to surface • Paying attention to the unique ways God communicates with you • Acting on the counsel you receive

"Checked Out"

When we are "checked out", we are not present at all; being "checked out" is akin to being in a hypnotic state. We become oblivious to our thoughts, our surroundings and our actions until something happens to shake us out of our hypnotic state.

We tend to become "checked out" when we are doing something we have done countless times before, which no longer requires us to maintain an attentive state. For example, recall a time you got in your car and drove a familiar route to a destination to which you frequently traveled. Have you ever found yourself suddenly arriving at your destination with no remembrance of what happened after you turned the key in the ignition? If you have, you were "checked out."

Being "checked out" happens to us all the time – when we are daydreaming, making plans and lists in our head or doing any of a number of the things we do on a daily basis that don't require us to be fully present.

Habitual Listening

Habitual listening refers to the automatic manner in which we typically relate to or tune into our inner dialogue. Most of us can recognize the little voice in our head. We have even heard the little voice as we have engaged in the process of thinking. However, part of our design as human beings is to live in an unconscious conditioned state of inattentiveness to the constant bombardment of thoughts that infiltrate our minds.

By living in a state of inattention to our internal dialogue, however, we miss the opportunity to reflectively examine the nature and the content of our thoughts. Inattention causes us to construct lives that are designed within our unconscious, unexamined and unchallenged assumptions and "truths." Inside this boundary, the possibility of living creative, vibrant lives is greatly diminished.

Being "checked out" and habitual listening illustrate how we relate to ourselves when we are operating in *automatic mode*. Automatic mode is the place we "live", so to speak, when we are not mindful of the present moment. As human beings, we live in the past – daydreaming, fantasizing about the way things were, remembering events from our past, taking actions based on past assumptions or unconscious rules we have devised to assist us in self-preservation.

The alternative to operating in automatic mode is to embrace a more intentional way of being in the approach we take to living our lives. Intention is a state of mind where we become more attentive, deliberate and aware. Becoming more mindful strengthens our resolve and our capacity to move toward a specific aim.

Intention represents purposeful action. Generative listening and sacred listening characterize a way of being wherein we relate to our internal dialogue with an intention to call into existence a new relationship with ourselves. Our capacity to listen to ourselves more intentionally results in a more creative and gratifying future for ourselves.

Generative Listening

Generative listening arises as the result of our choice to become more aware of our internal dialogue. Generative listening requires that we take a stand to create a future for ourselves that is not an extension of our past; it is an intentional conscious commitment to **generate** a new way of listening to ourselves.

At the heart of generative listening is the intention to listen to our thoughts with greater attentiveness. As we become more adept at paying attention to our internal dialogue, our awareness grows, enabling us to examine the content of our thoughts and question the validity and truth of what we hear.

In my story at the beginning of this chapter, I found myself in a state of great suffering and despair. As I became conscious of my thoughts, I heard myself saying that the situation was too much for me to bear, that I was alone in the world and that no one could help me. In the moment that I recognized that my thoughts were responsible for driving me into even deeper states of despair, I found the strength to question the veracity of what I was telling myself. I ultimately replaced the messages of despair with messages of affirmation such as: "I am a strong woman," "God never gives us more than we can handle," "I have family and friends who love me," "God can help me, etc." The affirming messages led me to the proactive actions to pray, to ask for help and to release my assessment of myself as a friendless, helpless woman who could be broken by the challenges of life.

Greater awareness provides us with the opportunity to replace old messages with more affirming messages that empower us to take greater risks to move toward the desired future that awaits us.

In my story above, the risk I took was that of releasing an old message brought with me from childhood into adulthood – a message saying that I was helpless, weak and alone. In releasing the old message, I made a commitment to approach life's challenges by finding within me a place of inner strength and relying on God as my Silent Partner. The risk was that of abandoning the familiar and comfortable (even though it was ineffective) in favor of a commitment that I didn't know I could actualize.

Greater awareness also allows us to become intimately acquainted with the mechanism of our mind and how it impacts our emotions. As a result of watching my internal dialogue, my emotions and my behavior, I was able to see that the thoughts I entertained contributed to my grief. Once I realized that, I could then choose to interrupt and shift the internal dialogue rather than continue to allow the flow of negative and debilitating thoughts into my consciousness.

Generative listening is a choice we make to intervene in the direction in which our lives are headed when we realize that that direction is inconsistent with our deepest desires for our lives.

Sacred Listening

Sacred listening is an intentional way of listening that requires us to pay attention to all our senses as we learn to discern the unique ways we receive messages from God. Sacred listening can only occur in silence and when we are in a receptive, open state of mind.

As human beings, we experience the world through our senses. Each of us has a preferred way in which we take in or perceive information from the outside world; we are predominantly visual, auditory or kinesthetic.

In her book, *The Intuitive Way*, Penney Peirce eloquently describes the three ways in which our intuition presents itself to us:

Modes of Human Perception	Characteristics
Visual Mode: Vision	• Tendency to trust what is seen over what is heard or felt • Pictures and sights • Dreams, daydreams, meditation, an image in the mind's eye • Realizations or insights that come after seeing or reading something
Auditory Mode: Voice	• Tendency to trust what is heard over what is felt or seen • Sounds and subtleties in sounds • The little voice you hear in your head • Insights that come after hearing something (music, conversations) • Sensitivity to the tone in people's voices
Kinesthetic Mode: Vibration	• Tendency to trust what is felt over what is seen or heard • Tactile feelings and visceral emotions • Physical sensations • Having a "gut" feeling about something

You can learn what your preferred sensory mode is by paying attention to the words you choose to use in every day conversation.

- People who are more visual tend to use visual language like: "I see what you mean."

29

- People who are more auditory tend to use auditory language like: "I hear you."
- People who are more kinesthetic tend to use kinesthetic language like: "I feel…"

It is important to note here that one's preferred mode is simply that – an unconscious preference. It does not mean that we are unable to process information through our other senses. We use all of our senses based on the situation or context in which we find ourselves, but we tend to rely more heavily on the sense we prefer most. By overusing our preferred sensory mode, we develop the ability to discern more subtleties in that mode until we have more life experiences that open up our other modalities.

Our emphasis in this chapter is on the auditory mode and how we can attune ourselves to listening to God's Voice, which we refer to as sacred listening and **Listening with the Heart**. The first condition for listening with the heart is that we slow down. It is important to set aside sufficient time for solitude and reflection where we will be uninterrupted.

During our solitude and reflection time, our focus is on reaching a state of inner calm, surrendering our control and desire to receive the answers or the outcomes we want, and learning how to perceive God's Voice amidst the myriad other internal messages in our consciousness. In our quiet state with our heart focused on God, thoughts, ideas, impressions, and visions will begin to enter our mind and heart.

The second condition for listening with the heart is that we engage in a consistent practice of acting on the counsel we receive. Not all messages we receive come from God. They often come from our hope and desire for a specific outcome. Through the practice of acting on the direction we receive, we become more discerning. Discernment is our capacity to keenly perceive what is typically hidden from our view. Unless we act on the information we receive, we will be unable to learn how to discern God's Voice. Taking successful action provides us with confirmation that the messages we receive are from God.

Developing Discernment

Sharpened Focus + Watchfulness + Insight + Action

One technique for developing discernment follows:

1. Select a time and place that will allow you to be reflective and undisturbed for 15 – 20 minutes.
2. On a piece of paper, write down a question relating to an area in which you need guidance.
3. As thoughts arise in your mind, write them down. Note any body sensations or visual signs that occur.
4. When you record a thought that "feels right" or "sounds right" to you or receive a visual sign that "looks right" to you, record the action you will take based on the counsel you receive.
5. Take action.
6. Evaluate the results.

As you practice this technique on a consistent basis, you will learn the specific ways that God communicates uniquely to you.

At a particularly difficult time in my life, I asked God for help with my grief. As I received loving messages from God, I was also counseled to reach out and ask for help. I was led to call my mother-in-law and, despite the fact that we were not close at that time, I immediately phoned her. As I talked and cried, my mother-in-law listened to me in a consoling and understanding manner. She opened up her own heart and shared her strength with me. In that time of my darkness, we achieved a level of closeness that continued to grow over the years.

WISDOM FROM THE AGES

A Man In Search Of His Luck

Once there was a man (we'll call him Anton) who was so unlucky that he was famous for being successful at failing. He made a mess of everything he tried to do. One day in a moment of deep despair, he threw up his hands in frustration and said to his friends "I am going to go to get some luck."

His friends scoffed and said "Don't be silly, Anton, you can't go and get luck. It isn't something you buy in a shop."

He said, "I can. I can go and get some luck. I know where to get it."

They asked, "Where?"

Anton replied, "God's got some. In fact God's got a lot and I am going to go and see God to find out how much I can have. I am not going to be greedy. I am only going to ask for about a bucketful."

They said "Don't be silly, Anton, you don't know where God is."

Anton confidently said, "I do. He lives in a house on the far side of the great forest."

Well, they mocked him and they ridiculed him relentlessly, but it didn't matter. He was determined. Thus, one morning he set off into the woods to see God. He had almost reached the trees when he met a wolf that was in horrible condition. Its eyes were red-rimmed and its ribs showed through its skin. It was very, very ill...very ill.

The wolf looked at Anton (this was back in the days when wolves could talk to men) and said, "Oh, can you help me please? I feel so ill."

Anton replied, "I'm sorry, I am very sorry, I can't help you. I'm on the way to God to get some luck."

"Oh, er, could you ask him for some for me, please?"

"Oh, yes" he said. "You are one of God's creatures; I am sure he will have some for you, yes, oh yes." Anton traveled on. Halfway through the forest he came upon a twisted and bent and gnarled tree.

The tree looked at him (this was back in the days when trees could talk to men) and the tree said, "Aah, can you help me please? I've got a terrible pain in my feet."

Anton replied, "I'm very sorry. I can't help you; I'm in a hurry. I'm going to God to get some luck."

The tree said "Aah, can you ask him for some for me please?"

Anton said, "Oh, I'm sure he will have some for you. Of course, yes."

Anton traveled on. Reaching the far edge of the trees, Anton walked out into the sunlight and happened upon a huge white tower. Halfway up the tower was a window. Sitting in the window was the most beautiful girl he had ever seen in his life.

The beautiful woman looked down at Anton (this was back in the days when girls could talk to men) and she said, "Oh please can you help me. I am so miserable; I am so unhappy."

He said, "I would love to stay and help you but I haven't got time. I am going to God to get some luck, you see."

"Oh" she said "could you ask him for some for me please?"

"Of course" he said, "I'm sure he'll have plenty for you, yes, ha ha, oh yes. See you when I come back."

Finally reaching God's House, Anton went in and saw God seated on a chair at the far end of a long room. Anton gingerly approached God and said, "God, I've come."

God said, "Anton, I know why you have come. You have come for some luck and I am going to help you."

Anton replied, "Oh I am so grateful. Thank you very, very much. I, er, I'm not greedy, I just want about a bucketful."

And God said, "Well, I am not going to give you any but I will tell you where it is.

Anton looked around the room quizzically and said, "Okay, where do you keep it?"

God said, "Well there is none in here. But, go home and just keep your eyes open because luck is all around you. All you have to do is to keep your eyes open and you will find it."

Well Anton thought that was rather an odd thing to say because he didn't walk around with his eyes shut. And he had never seen any lumps of luck lying around anywhere. And so he said "Oh, okay. Well, perhaps, could you just start me off with a handful, just to get me going?"

God shook his head.

"Well" he said, "just er, just a bit to fill a pocket, sort of?"

God shook his head again.

"Well" he said "how about a pinch of luck just to get me started? No. No, it's all around me, I just have to keep my eyes open."

God nodded and said, "That's right."

As Anton turned to go, he remembered the wolf and the tree and the girl and he told God about them and God told him what to say. So he set off back home feeling very disconsolate. He wasn't very happy with God. He felt God had let him down because he could have just given him some luck. It wouldn't have been too much trouble. Just a little bit. And all he had said was "It's all around you, just keep your eyes open." What a silly thing to say!

He reached the tower and saw the gorgeous girl still sitting in the window. She looked down at him, and said "Oh, hello. Did you see God?"

"Oh yes, I did, yes."

"What did he say about me?"

"Oh" he said, "what you've got to do is find a handsome, unattached young man, fall in love and get married. You will be happy for the rest of your life."

"Oh, I see. I, er, I think you are very handsome. What do you think about me?"

"Oh" he said, "I think you are absolutely beautiful."

"Oh thank you. Um, are you, er, are you married?"

"No, no, I am not married, no."

"Have you got a girlfriend?"

"No, I haven't got a girlfriend."

"Would you like a girlfriend?"

"Oh, I'd love a girlfriend."

"Would you like a girlfriend like me?"

"Oh, I would LOVE a girlfriend like you. Ooooh!"

"Well, what about you and me getting together and being girlfriend and boyfriend?"

"Oh no" he said "no, I would love it, Oh I would love to be your boyfriend but you see, I'm looking for my luck and God said it is all around me. I just have to keep my eyes open. I am so sorry. I can't stay. Oh, I would love to stay but I haven't got the time. I am sorry."

Anton went on. He had gone half way through the forest when he encountered the tree. "Aah hello. Did you see God?" asked the tree.

Anton said, "Oh yes, I saw God. He said the reason you have a pain in your feet is that there is a metal box under your taproot. The box is full of gold and your root can't get through it. That's what's giving you the pain. All you have to do is dig out the box".

And the tree said, "Well, I'm a tree and while we trees can talk, we can't dig, but over there is a shovel. You could do it for me."

"Oh no" he said "no, no. You see I am looking for my luck and it is all around me. I just have to keep my eyes open. I haven't got time to dig." And he went on.

He reached the far edge of the trees and saw the wolf looking even worse than before. It looked very, very, very, very ill. The wolf looked at Anton and said, "Ooh, did you see God? What did he say about me?"

Anton said, "Oh, your problem is an easy one. The only thing wrong with you is that you're hungry. God said what you've got to do is to jump on the first silly fool that comes along and eat him."

And that's exactly what the wolf did.

KEY THOUGHTS

In our story about Anton, we can presume that there was something in the way he listened to himself that caused him to be closed off to the possibility of creating a successful life for himself. While we were not specifically privy to his thoughts in the story, we can see that Anton listened to himself in an habitual way that blinded him to the cues in his environment that reflected God's wisdom.

Anton was so oblivious to his thoughts and feelings about his actions that he failed to question the intended meaning of the phrase "Luck is all around you" and instead followed a predetermined path based on his own limited interpretations.

Another element of Anton's downfall is that he suffered from the disease of "busyness." On his way to see God, he was so busy hurrying and scurrying that he failed to be of genuine service to those around him who were in need. On his return trip from his visit to God, Anton traveled in such haste that he was too busy to see the keys to his own successful future right in front of him.

Nature of Our Internal Dialogue

Most people, unless they have been on the path of self-discovery or spiritual awareness for a while, live in a primary state of not being aware of their internal dialogue. They are aware that they have thoughts, but they rarely become conscious of them such that they can examine the nature of those thoughts and the ways in which they influence their feeling states, attitudes, mindsets and, ultimately, their actions.

The thoughts that comprise our internal dialogue are myriad. To examine this idea for yourself, once again turn your attention inward and do the following exercise for at least five minutes.

Sitting Exercise I: Focus on Your Breathing

- Find a quiet location and sit comfortably in a chair.
- Sit upright, place your feet firmly on the floor and rest your hands comfortably in your lap.
- Close your eyes, take a few deep breaths, release any tension in your body and relax.
- For the next five minutes, simply focus on your breath. Follow it with your attention as you inhale and exhale.
- When you notice your attention wandering, gently bring your focus back to your breath.

If you are new to this kind of exercise, you will discover how difficult it actually is to keep your attention focused on your breath. You will experience for yourself how much "chatter" there is in your mind.

You will also notice that your thoughts come unbidden like a thief in the night to steal your attention from the present moment.

There is nothing we need do to summon our thoughts; they are always there. They come and they go without any assistance from us. We live in a torrent of thoughts and impressions – whether we are aware of them or not – that invade our attention and operate in the background of our minds like a radio broadcasting 24 hours a day.

Let's try another experiment…

Sitting Exercise II: Observe Your Thoughts

- Find a quiet location and sit comfortably in a chair.
- Sit upright, place your feet firmly on the floor and rest your hands comfortably in your lap.
- Close your eyes, take a few deep breaths, release any tension in your body and relax.
- For the next five minutes, simply notice your thoughts. Let them arise and fade away with the inhalation and exhalation of your breath.
- Don't force anything. Imagine that each thought is like a balloon. Watch it as it floats past you and disappears and notice the next thought that arises.
- To the extent that you can, try not to hold onto any of the thoughts, just notice them and let them fall away.

Take a moment to consider the thoughts that arose in your mind.

- What did you notice about them?
- What did you discover about the nature of your thoughts?

Habitual Self-Talk

Our thoughts generally consist of future plans; things we need to remember to do; complaining or whining about something; reliving something that happened in the past; anticipating or dreading something that will be taking place in the future; criticism about what we should or shouldn't have done, regrets, etc.

Our internal messages are designed to help us navigate successfully in the world. They are evaluative and often critical in nature. We are constantly analyzing, judging and criticizing the world and the people around us as well as analyzing, judging and criticizing our own actions and feelings.

Our internal voice combines parental and social feedback that helps us determine the appropriate boundaries inside of which we think we need to operate to be safe from shame and harm, and to be accepted by others. From the feedback we receive throughout our lives, we make up rules about what we should and should not do, the kind of person we should become, what behaviors are acceptable and unacceptable based on our observations of what gets rewarded and what gets punished, etc.

In essence, the function of this voice is self-preservation. It operates largely unconsciously – until such time that we become more aware – and dictates our actions and the choices we make. We refer to this unconscious, subtle voice as *habitual self-talk*. Habitual self-talk is the way our internal world operates unless it is interrupted by a more intentional voice and replaced with more affirming messages.

Habitual self-talk is constraining. It limits our ability to live truly creative, out-of-the-box lives because it operates unconsciously to ensure that we live within very specific boundaries we have devised to stay safe in the world.

Generative Self-Talk

Through the process of self-discovery and inner exploration we become awakened to our internal world and we experience directly how pervasive it is in influencing the choices we make. Awareness is key to transforming our lives. As we become more aware, we gain access to the skills that enable us to interrupt our habitual self-talk.

Awareness is the ability to step outside of ourselves and to watch ourselves dispassionately – without judgment. As we learn to recognize and turn the volume up on our habitual self-talk, we can then more consciously examine the thoughts that arise. In examining our thoughts, we place ourselves in a better position to question the assumptions that surface about who we are. From this place, we can re-shape unfavorable messages by replacing them with affirmations and develop a greater capacity to make authentic choices that evolve from a reflective way of being.

We call this kind of internal dialogue generative self-talk. Generative self-talk requires that we engage in practices that build our capacity to become more aware. It also requires that we consciously choose to examine and work with our internal dialogue – listening to what we say and how we say it – and install affirmative messages. Self-observation exercises, various modalities of therapy, meditation, journaling, mindfulness activities, affirmations, etc. are among the many disciplines in which we can engage to retrain our self-talk.

Generative self-talk expands our possibilities and promotes more proactive behavior, granting us an internal power that supports us in generating a more intentional future for ourselves.

Sacred Communication

Sacred communication is not about how we talk to ourselves or manage our internal dialogue. Rather, it refers to the communication that occurs between God and us and the connection that allows us to discern God's Voice from among the many other voices which stream through our consciousness.

Sacred communication becomes possible in stillness, when we are calm, centered and at peace. However, unlike self-talk (either habitual or generative), sacred communication is what we would term a whole-body phenomenon. We receive sacred communication as a voice, a vision, a vibration or any combination thereof.

Sacred communication, like generative self-talk, requires that we develop an awareness of our internal dialogue; it also involves us becoming more aware of the unique ways we receive both intuition and inspiration.

Receiving God's Voice

God speaks to us in a still small voice we can only hear when we become silent and take the time to be in communion with Him. It is, therefore, ironic that we have been designed in such a way that the loudest voice we hear in our mind contains distracting thoughts of past memories, future plans, anxieties and fears all clamoring for our attention. Because of the way we are designed, we must become exceptionally purposeful and resolute in overcoming our wiring to develop a state of being that produces a receptive mind.

We live mostly in the past or the future and rarely find ourselves in the present moment – which is where God lives – unless we intentionally develop our ability to be mindful. God lives in the Now moment and speaks to us in the Now moment.

It is not the nature of the human mind to be centered in the present moment. We live in the past: daydreaming, fantasizing, and harboring regrets. We live in the future: planning, wishing, dreaming and fearing the unknown that has yet to materialize (and indeed may never). When we look objectively at the content of our thoughts, we can see that our present, our Now, is filled with either what has happened (past) or what we imagine will happen (future).

It is when we are receptive, open and still that we are empowered to enter into two-way communication with God. Some call this kind of communication two-way prayer because through the desires of our heart we seek direction and guidance from God and receive His answer as a result of our deepened receptivity and earnestness.

Sacred communication requires that we listen purposefully but differs from generative self-talk in that our intention is to connect more consciously to God by resting in stillness and simply receiving the more sacred loving messages that flow to us.

Inspiration

Sacred communication also incorporates the idea of allowing ourselves to be influenced – or inspired – by God. Inspiration literally represents the act of drawing in God's Spirit in a manner in which our emotions or intellect are elevated, stimulated or quickened.

We prepare ourselves to be in sacred communication with God, by coming to the relationship with a willingness to be influenced, a spirit of surrender and a clear intention to act on the messages we receive. In so doing, we learn over time how to clearly discern God's Voice and how best to align our will with God's Will for us.

Characteristics of Internal Dialogue

Automatic	
"Checked Out"	**Habitual Self-Talk**
• Unconscious • Hypnotic	• Primarily unconscious, passive • Helps us operate effectively within the unconscious rules we think are vital to our survival • Critical, evaluative, judgmental • Designed for self-preservation • Contains survival-oriented messages • Constraining; Often saps power and effectiveness • Leads to reactive behavior

Intentional	
Generative Self-Talk	**Sacred Communication**
• Requires conscious choice	• Arises from being present, calm and at peace
• Contains affirmative messages that interrupt habitual self-talk	• A whole-body phenomenon
	• Requires an open heart and receptive way of being
• Purposeful: Springs from a commitment to create a more satisfying future	• Centering: Fosters deeper, more conscious connection to spirit
• Expanding: Grants power and effectiveness	• Contains loving messages
• Leads to proactive behavior	• Transforming: Helps align human will with God's will
	• Leads to inspired behavior

CONNECTING TO THE SPIRITUAL

In listening with the heart, we open ourselves to receive a different level of wisdom and understanding than that which extends from our past conditioning. It requires us to become alert to our senses and the unique ways we receive messages from God.

Listening with the Heart – The Process

1. Listening with the heart begins first with our passionate desire for connection with God as we turn our attention inward. We approach the connection with an attitude of faith and trust

2. Next, we focus on achieving a relaxed state of mind and body. Deep, slow breathing helps us clear our surface thoughts and release the tension from our bodies. In reaching a calmer internal state, we are then able to go deeper into our inner sanctuary.

3. From within our inner sanctuary, we open our heart to God and converse with God about His will for our lives or about any situation or problem confronting us. At this point, we allow ourselves to be fully present to the situation just as it is. We allow our thoughts, feelings, fears and hopes to arise without trying to manage them.

4. When the flow of thoughts and impressions begins to slow down, record the thoughts, visions and feelings that occur in the stillness. Then examine what you have written through the following lens:
   - Is the prescribed course of action honest, loving, pure, unselfish?
   - Is the prescribed course of action in line with your duties to God, self, family?
   - Is the prescribed course of action consistent with your espoused values?
   - Is the prescribed course of action in line with your understanding of the highest spiritual principles?

5. At certain times, we may feel that we haven't received any specific information. However, listening with the heart becomes a filter for our awareness as we explore all around us what God is trying to convey to us. If we continue to maintain an attentive way of being, we may discover the answers through dreams, songs that we hear, something we read, conversations with others, etc. We just need to look to find the answers that are all around us.

6. The last step is to act on what we discover and evaluate the results we achieve. It may be that at times we fail to accurately discern God's true message and carry out actions that don't succeed. With God's help, however, we can turn our failures into learning and growth opportunities that serve us in the long term. At other times, our actions may result in opposition from others, especially when we are attempting to bring something new into existence. It is important to remember that opposition does not always signal that we are on the wrong track. It may simply mean that those around us are uncomfortable with our growth or

our choices. In these instances, it is important to pray and ask God to help that person to find peace in his or her heart and to help you move forward with faith and courage.

PERSONAL MEDITATION

As you become acquainted with the content of your thoughts and your habitual internal dialogue, you can delve into them more deeply by engaging in the following two-stage process. Using the guidelines in **Sitting Exercise II: Observe Your Thoughts**, examine each thought carefully and ask yourself the following questions for each thought you surface:

Stage One
- Is it true?
- Is it kind?
- Is it helpful?

You may want to record each thought to analyze how it makes you feel and to determine emerging patterns. Those thoughts that empower us fulfill each criterion in Stage One.

In Stage Two, you will replace each thought that disempowers you with an affirmative thought. Write out each affirmative thought on an index card and review it regularly throughout the day. You might even post your cards on your bathroom mirror, your refrigerator and anywhere else to retrain your mind.

Stage Two
Replace your debilitating or disempowering thoughts with affirmative and loving messages and repeat them over throughout your day until you feel the "grip" of your old thoughts loosening.

SERVING OTHERS
How to Be Available

As we become more skillful in learning to listen with our heart, we become a valuable partner for anyone else on the path of achieving greater spiritual insight. Our lives become a model for what's possible for others as they grow toward becoming more spiritually connected individuals.

As we begin to live our lives in a more centered, loving, and relaxed way, the aura of peace envelops us. This inner light enables us to bring peace to the situations and people around us by our mere presence.

By living two-way prayer, we can serve others by making ourselves available as a sounding board to them as they practice living out God's message. As a result of the wisdom we have gained through our personal experiences, we may be able to help another see God's plan for his or her life more clearly than he or she can in isolation.

PUTTING IT ALL TOGETHER

There is no better way to reinvent ourselves than to learn how to release ourselves from the constraining thoughts that hold us hostage to a self and a life that is conditioned by our habitual internal dialogue. An internal dialogue that is designed for self-preservation obscures our view of a creative, fulfilling future self and future life.

Intervening in our thought process through the intentional listening modes of Generative Listening and Listening with the Heart develops our capacity to become more mindful and aware, thereby equipping us with the tools to create lives of purpose and joy.

Chapter Three

Expand Your Willingness to Surrender

PERSONAL REFLECTION

I have had several significant moments of surrender in my life. One of the most notable of these moments occurred when I surrendered my alcoholism and drug addiction to a power greater than myself. When I made the decision to attend a drug and alcohol treatment center, I thought it was the most important decision I would need to make to get my life back in control.

What I had not anticipated was that I would also be required to attend Alcoholics Anonymous meetings every week. Besides the fact that I didn't believe attendance at those meetings was necessary, within myself I initially resisted that level of interference in my life. However, having no choice in the matter, I capitulated.

After attending AA for two years, I came to realize and experience for myself that AA is a serious program of spiritual transformation. As I began to earnestly practice the Twelve Steps, I learned how to live a sober and fulfilling life. The Twelve Steps provided me with a structure that has helped me learn how to maintain a daily conscious connection with God and has transformed me into a spirit-filled woman of character and service.

In 2005, I will celebrate the 20th anniversary of the first day of my entry into the world of sober living. Over the past 20 years, I have seen many people unsuccessfully attempt to find their way from the darkness of addiction to the light of recovery. I believe that a large part of the reason for failing to recover has to do with an inability to fully comprehend and embrace the Twelve Steps.

My premise is that people fail to maintain a continuous program of recovery because they are unsuccessful in grasping the very first of the Twelve Steps, which begins with some version of: "I admit I am powerless and that my life has become unmanageable." In my mind, the first step is the most critical step because it requires that we choose surrender at one of the most crucial turning points in our life and establishes how we will allow ourselves to be influenced by the remaining steps. Admitting our powerlessness is the first important act of surrender because it requires that we take the emotional step of surrendering the idea that we are ever in control. Implicit in the acceptance of our own powerlessness is the suggestion that we will learn how to live a surrendered life.

In my own personal journey, I found that I had to examine and solidify my relationship with God to take that first step authentically. I discovered that the capacity to surrender is directly related to our relationship with God. If our relationship with God is weak, surrender becomes impossible. If we harbor doubts about God's role in our life, we resist the notion that surrender is a viable way to relate to circumstances over which we have no control in our lives.

Surrender requires faith in the goodness of life and trust in God. At the time I first began to grapple with the issue of surrender in my own life, I came to the important and pivotal realization that I didn't trust God. I had to admit that truth to myself in order to repair my erroneous assumptions about God's role in my life up to that moment in time. As I earnestly reviewed my life with all its most challenging aspects, the pattern of God's hand in my life was striking.

I also came to understand that any fear about surrendering my future to God came from knowing that I wouldn't always get my way. Abandoning the idea that I had any real control of my life demanded that I learn to cultivate an attitude of open-minded willingness to follow a spiritual direction rather than an ego-driven direction in my life.

LOOKING INWARD

Surrender is an act of readiness to freely turn our human will over to Divine Will. Surrender as a spiritual practice helps us develop an approach to life from a place of deep inner strength and faith. As we become more mature in our spiritual practice, we become more adept at relinquishing our need to control people, situations and outcomes. When we no longer feel the need to exert control in our lives, we develop the willingness and the capacity to allow ourselves instead to be guided by Spirit.

In looking at the big problems in our lives, it is readily apparent where we might benefit from an act of surrender. However, opportunities to surrender also appear to us in any situation where we find ourselves struggling. For so many of us, despite how big or how small our trials may be, surrender is never easy.

When we're suffering and have nowhere else to go, surrender becomes the obvious choice to make. Yet, sometimes, even under the most trying circumstances, we resist relinquishing our control. Then there are those times when we refuse to accept the reality of our circumstances and make every attempt to impose our will to change what ultimately cannot be changed.

As you examine the intractable circumstances in your life, consider the following questions:

- What situations have you been putting up with or trying to change?
- How have you tried to resolve these situations?
- What was the outcome(s)?
- Are you satisfied with the outcome(s)
- What do you need to let go of in order to achieve a state of surrender in these situations?
- What is stopping you from letting go?

Drawing from his lifelong personal search for purpose to become one of the world's greatest modern mythologists, Joseph Campbell said, "We must be willing to let go of the life we have planned, so as to have the life that is waiting for us."

WISDOM FROM THE AGES

The Story Of The Sage Of Herat

At the time of Sultan Mahmud of Ghazna there lived a young man by the name of Haidar Ali Jan. His father, Iskandar Khan, decided to obtain the patronage of the sultan for his son, so he sent Haidar Ali away to study spiritual matters under a very famous sage. When Haidar Ali had mastered his spiritual studies, his father took him into the presence of the sultan.

"Mighty Sultan," said Iskandar Khan, "I have had this youth, my eldest and most intelligent son, specially trained in our spiritual ways, so that he might obtain a worthy position at your Majesty's court, knowing that you are a patron of learning!"

The sultan did not look up, but just said, "Bring him back in a year!"

Slightly disappointed, but nursing high hopes, Iskandar Khan sent Haidar Ali to study the works and visit the shrines of the great spiritual masters of the past so that the intervening time would not be wasted.

The next year, when he took Haidar Ali back to the sultan's court, he said, "Oh, Wise One! My son has carried out long and arduous journeys, and at the same time added to his knowledge of our spiritual ways. Please have him tested, so it can be proved that he will be of great service to your Majesty's court."

"Let him," said the sultan immediately, "return after another year!"

During the next twelve months, Haidar Ali traveled much throughout many lands and gained even greater spiritual depth. When he returned to the court, the sultan took one look at him and said, "He may care to come back after a further year!"

Haidar Ali made the pilgrimage to the holy land that year. He consulted rare books and never missed an opportunity to seek out and pay his respects to the great living spiritual teachers of the time.

When he returned to Ghazna, Sultan Mahmud said to him, "Now select a spiritual teacher, if he will have you, and come back in a year!"

Another year was over and Iskandar Khan prepared to take his son to the court; however, this time Haidar Ali showed no interest in going there. He sat at the feet of his teacher in Herat, and nothing that his father could say would move him.

"I have wasted my time and my money, and this young man has failed the tests imposed by the sultan," Iskandar Khan lamented. He decided to abandon his plan and left Haidar Ali with his teacher.

Meanwhile, the day when Haidar Ali was due to present himself came and went. Sultan Mahmud said to his courtiers, "Prepare yourselves for a visit to Herat, there is someone there whom I have to see."

As the sultan's horse-drawn carriages entered Herat to the sound of trumpets, Haidar Ali's teacher took him to the nearby sanctuary, and they waited. Shortly afterwards, Sultan Mahmud and his courtier, taking off their shoes, presented themselves at the sanctuary.

"Here, Sultan Mahmud," said the spiritual teacher, "is the man who was nothing while he was a visitor of kings, but who is now one who is visited by kings, Take him as your spiritual counselor, for he is ready!"

This story is a wonderful allegory that illustrates how we might approach surrender as a spiritual practice in our own lives. Several key points arise in this story about what is required for us to live a surrendered life.

The most dominant message in the story of Haidar Ali is the importance of paying attention to and acting upon the counsel we receive. We see, first, Haidar Ali embracing his father's desire that he seek a position with the sultan for which he trained and studied his entire life. Next we see the consistency of his efforts in following the will of the sultan, who repeatedly sent him away with further instructions that Haidar Ali ultimately obeyed.

One of the subtlest distinctions we see in the story is Haidar Ali's shift from submissiveness to a true surrendered way of being. Throughout the story we see that Haidar Ali essentially suppressed his own will to that of the sultan in order to reap the personal reward of future employment. This was an act of submission. As Haidar Ali continued to engage in the <u>process</u> of spiritual development with less focus on the <u>prize</u> of attaining a certain outcome, he realized a genuine surrendered way of being.

In our lives, God is like the sultan, who continually gives us opportunities to follow His will, not out of fear or thought of future gain, but as an exchange for gaining something greater than anything we can imagine, plan or hope for.

Surrender entails a willingness to listen to the sacred messages we receive with an intention to act on that counsel. As we develop in our capacity to live a surrendered life, our focus shifts from **having** to **being**. Surrender is about the process, not the prize – the process of becoming, not the prize of attaining.

KEY THOUGHTS

We often find it difficult to approach life with a surrendered attitude because, we have an unresolved relationship with God. During these times, it is important not to overlook the power of asking those questions in our lives that cause us to reflect deeply on issues of highest importance to us. In my case, I had never stopped to ask myself "Do I trust God?" This was an important question for me because I had always espoused my trust in God but hadn't seen that the way I related to the circumstances in my life contradicted what I told myself.

In considering the possibility of admitting powerlessness in managing my own life, I had a visceral reaction of resistance to the idea. I vividly remember my internal conversation, which went something like this…

> "Well, if I'm powerless, who's going to be in control of my life? They say that God is, but I'm not so sure I like the idea of God being in control. Why is that? Because I don't trust where He's going to take me."

I was surprised to hear myself admit that I didn't trust God, but that insight led me to understand that my relationship with God was insufficient at that time. It became immediately clear that unless I established a stronger relationship with Him, hope for a better, more inspired future would be lost to me.

Another reason we find it difficult to live a surrendered life is because of our perception that surrender is an act of cowardice and weakness. We don't discern the true power of a surrendered way of being. Surrender, which emanates from a place of strength, is not the same as submission, which arises from weakness.

As shown on the following page, surrender is the state of being that falls between submission and control.

Submission	Surrender	Control
• Involves suppression or sacrifice of one's will in favor of another's in order to achieve personal reward or to satisfy a need for self-preservation • Implies domination by another • Giving up or giving in as a result of being overwhelmed or overpowered • Power situation in which one party wields power over another • The weaker willed one places itself under control of the stronger willed one • Passivity	• An active process of conscious, courageous choice wherein we do have to give up *something* in exchange for something greater than we could have imagined, planned or even hoped for • Connection to something greater than ego and sense of self-importance • An orientation to life that is open, accepting and trusting • Involves maintaining our intention and engaging fully but letting go of any expectation that things will go the way we had planned or expected • Includes an element of detachment	• Provides an illusion of safety, security and certainty • Focus is on forcing things to conform to our desired outcomes • Requires us to exert our willpower • Arises from our attachment to the results

A surrendered way of being is developed in partnership with God, and places God in the center of our lives as the only true source of our power and internal strength.

CONNECTING TO THE SPIRITUAL

Surrender is a spiritual choice that connects us to God in four distinct ways:

1. **Release:** Letting Go
    - What's not working
    - Struggle
    - Expectations, resentments and regrets

    Surrender as *release* means that we let go of the things that are not working in our lives, including those areas in which we find ourselves struggling. We also let go of the unfulfilled expectations, resentments and regrets that cause us to suffer. In release, we let go of our emotional attachment that situations will turn out as we hope they will. Sometimes release means that we need to take specific actions to end our relationship with things that create negativity in our lives such as abusive relationships, dead-end careers and our preconceived ideas about how people and situations should be.

2. **Relinquishing Control:** Turning Over
    - Difficult situations and problems
    - Stop grasping and striving

    Surrender as *relinquishing control* means that we turn over the resolution of difficult situations and problems to God. When we notice that our aggressive measures are alienating others and wreaking havoc in our lives or in our spirit, we also stop grasping, striving and pushing to achieve a specific outcome. Relinquishing control often requires that we simply do nothing other than ask for help and wait in faith for a solution to present itself to us.

3. **Accepting:** Ceasing Resistance
    - Embracing the way things are
    - Open hands, open heart

Surrender as **accepting** means that we accept the things we cannot change by embracing them the way they are. Acceptance requires that we see situations as they are and not as we wish them to be. Accepting people and situations as they are allows us to be fully available and present with open hands (receptivity) and an open heart (trust).

4. **Surrender as Spiritual Practice:** Way of Being

Surrender as **spiritual practice** means that we choose to live a surrendered life. We develop a way of being wherein we approach life with a sense of faith, trust, and humility. With humility we ask for guidance and direction whenever we embark on any new endeavor. With humility we ask for human and spiritual help when and where we need it. We listen with our hearts for God's answers and we follow the guidance we receive with a trusting, courageous and grateful heart.

PERSONAL MEDITATION

As we learn to harness the power of surrender in our lives, one of the most powerful meditations we can engage in is to focus our minds on the magnificence of God and our hearts on the presence of God within and around us.

*   Find a quiet location and sit comfortably in a chair.
*   Sit upright, place your feet firmly on the floor and rest your hands comfortably in your lap.
*   Close your eyes, take a few deep breaths, release any tension in your body and relax.
*   For the next five minutes, simply focus on your love for God. As you focus on God, imagine a white light pouring into your heart area as you inhale.
*   Feel your heart expanding with God's love. As you exhale, imagine the light filling up your body.
*   When you notice your attention wandering, gently bring your attention back to your love for God.
*   Allow yourself to be bathed in the feeling of God's presence within you.

When you first begin meditating, you may have difficulty quieting and focusing your mind. This difficulty eases with long-time, ongoing practice, but inherent in any meditation practice is the "up and down experience." Sometimes you feel you are doing it well and other times you struggle. What is important in meditation is that you develop the discipline to do it consistently – preferably daily. Ideally, you will meditate for at least twenty minutes each session, but it may take you some time to achieve that goal. Be gentle and work up to the twenty-minute goal gradually. For the first couple of weeks, you may only be able to meditate for five minutes a day. Take it as slowly as you need to, emphasizing consistency over quality and quantity.

The above meditation will help you develop a powerful connection with God and enable you to more easily access His presence throughout your day.

SERVING OTHERS
How to Be Available

Through embracing surrender as a way of being and a way of approaching your difficulties and struggles, you will become a strong and powerful partner, sounding board and guide to others as they traverse their own spiritual journeys.

You will be able to share your experience with others about how to listen for and heed God's counsel. One of the most important ways you can serve others is by helping them recognize the power of surrender and how it differs from submitting out of fear or for hopes of future personal gain.

We are living in an era of excessive materialism where so many are searching for meaning and purpose. Living a surrendered life helps us radiate a beacon of inner light that attracts and makes us recognizable to those in need of spiritual support.

PUTTING IT ALL TOGETHER

The acts of surrendering and aligning our will with God's will for us are important choices in our quest to live a spirit-filled life. Together, our capacities to surrender, to listen with our heart and to carry out the counsel we receive comprise a potent transformational process that accelerates our spiritual development.

Do invest the time daily to cultivate a conscious connection with God that is strong enough to accompany you throughout your day. Meditate and pray to learn to stay open to God's presence in your life.

- Develop a spiritual practice that includes learning how to live a surrendered life.
- Examine your life and acknowledge the situations in which you find yourself stuck.
- Recognize specific people, situations, attitudes, feelings and thoughts that cause you to suffer.
- Identify situations you need to release, relinquish control over or accept.
- Develop sufficient humility to ask for and accept help from God and others.

Chapter Four

Take Yourself Off Autopilot

PERSONAL REFLECTION

I vividly recall the period in my life when I was intensely dissatisfied and unhappy. I wasn't having any fun, and life seemed like so much drudgery. I was just going through the motions, existing but not thriving; doing the things I was supposed to be doing, but not experiencing any satisfaction or joy.

In those days, my life was small. I didn't venture out to do anything that made me feel uncomfortable or that might have an unpredictable result. I tried to stay within the bounds of what was familiar, of what I knew. I defined myself by my likes and dislikes, my occupation, my habits and my roles. The only people in my life were my husband, a few friends and my husband's family.

When opportunities emerged for me to participate in unfamiliar, new or different activities, my automatic response would be to say "no." My biggest commitment at that time was to "being comfortable." Being comfortable meant that I stayed away from anything that made me feel anxious or unsure of myself. Being comfortable also meant that I wouldn't allow myself to have new learning experiences because I feared the risks I would have to take and I feared failing.

Over time, a realization crept into my life that represented the dawning of my awakening. I grasped that as long as I continued to say "no" to the blessings and invitations God was sending me, I would never have a life I loved. My attachment to being comfortable was slowly sapping the vitality out of a potentially joyous life. Once I acknowledged the damage I was inflicting on my own spirit, I immediately set out to change my life.

The most significant change I made was a small one – to start saying, "yes" to invitations to participate in activities that would teach me more about others and myself. That one action has motivated me to take risks I never thought I would take: learning to live life without anesthetizing myself, purchasing a house as a single woman, getting remarried, changing careers, contributing to my community through volunteer activities, starting my own business, etc. The list is long and still growing.

I have gained the courage to pursue my dreams because I have stopped allowing my feelings of fear or discomfort to hold me back. I might get slowed down a bit, but I continue to move forward. I now understand that saying "no" was simply a habit I automatically relied on to keep me safe in the world. Learning to live more consciously from my spiritual center has helped me take myself off autopilot. As a result, I have access to an unlimited source of strength, safety, and joy that fuels a spirit-filled life.

LOOKING INWARD

We limit ourselves by not recognizing that our preferences, tendencies, thoughts, beliefs, habits and actions imprison us unless we begin to ask deeper questions of ourselves, such as:

- What do I want?
- What experiences do I want to bring into my life?
- How can I make my life more meaningful?
- What am I grateful for?
- What's my purpose?
- What is life calling me to do?
- What brings me joy?
- What's stopping me from receiving God's blessings?

- What contributions do I want to make to my family/job/community?
- How am I stopping myself or holding myself back?

Asking deep questions of ourselves helps us to break through the patterns that compel us to act in certain ways, by shifting our perception of what is important.

I had to ask myself the question, "What is causing you to feel dissatisfied with your life?" Next, I had to take the time to seriously analyze my situation: to look at my patterns and my habits and to tell the truth about my responsibility in how my life had unfolded. Finally, I had to determine necessary actions to take myself off autopilot and intervene in my automatic and habitual behavior.

The following list describes some ways of being that create dissatisfaction and often compel us to operate on autopilot:

- Perfectionism, striving for high standards you can never achieve
- Putting the needs of others before your own and not attending to your own needs
- Constant busyness and attempts to maintain an image of success
- A perennial search for that which you think will bring you happiness and an inability to be satisfied with your accomplishments
- Lack of or limited involvement with others
- Constant skepticism and doubt
- Lack of focus, escape through variety of actions, tendency to see the world through rose-colored glasses
- Domineering control, inability to surrender
- Avoidance of uncomfortable situations

Where in your life are you living on autopilot? What small actions can you take to make a significant shift in your life?

WISDOM FROM THE AGES

The Story Of The Sleepy Man

There was once a good man by the name of Amyn. He had spent his whole life cultivating qualities that would eventually take him to Paradise. He gave freely to the poor and he loved his fellow creatures and served them. Remembering the need to have patience, he endured great and unexpected hardships, often for the sake of others. He made journeys in search of knowledge. His humility and exemplary behavior were such that his reputation as a wise man and good citizen resounded from the East to the West, and from the North to the South.

Amyn exercised all these qualities whenever he remembered to do so, but his one shortcoming was inattention. This tendency was not strong in him and he considered that, balanced against the other things which he did practice, it could only be regarded as a small fault.

Amyn was fond of sleep, and sometimes when he was asleep, opportunities to seek knowledge, or to understand it, or to practice real humility, or to add to the sum total of good behavior, passed him by and did not return. Just as the good qualities left their impression upon his essential self, so did the characteristic of inattention.

And then one day, Amyn died. Finding himself beyond this life, and making his way toward the doors of Paradise, he paused to examine his conscience. He felt that the qualities he had cultivated combined with his lifelong acts of virtuous behavior were enough to warrant his entry into Paradise.

The gates were shut, and then a voice addressed Amyn saying: "Be watchful, for the gates will open only once every hundred years!"

So, Amyn settled down to wait, excited at the prospect, but deprived of chances to exercise virtues towards humankind, he found his capacity of attention was not enough for him. After watching for what seemed like an age, his head nodded in sleep. For an instant his eyelids closed, and at that moment the gates yawned open. Before his eyes were fully open again, the doors closed, with a roar loud enough to wake the dead!

Taking yourself off autopilot means that you begin to awaken to the specific ways in which you have limited yourself from having a rich, vital and energizing life that is meaningful to you. Being awake requires that you become aware of and replace your self-limiting habits and that you break out of the trance of your conditioning.

KEY THOUGHTS

The common thread that runs throughout this book is that there are two ways of being: automatic/habitual and intentional/awake. Automatic behavior functions in two ways: first, as the formula we have put together to be safe, accepted and successful in the world, and, second, as a strategy for reacting to what occurs around us.

We have been taught – by family, educational systems, our religions, the communities to which we belong and society – what to believe, what is valuable, what is important, what is acceptable and appropriate; this teaching has been unconscious and pervasive.

When we act from our automatic, habitual patterns, it is as if we are operating on autopilot. We are not aware of what we really want; we just do what we think we are required to do, without awareness and without much thought. Dissatisfaction is a signal to us that our behavior and our choices stem from a place that is not nourishing our spirit.

So much of our lives is spent unconsciously waiting to see "how it will all turn out," not realizing that how it turns out is completely up to us (in partnership with Spirit) and not to our circumstances or to fate. Our lives cannot reach their fullest potential until we discover where we are living on autopilot and begin to live more intentionally.

Intentional behavior helps us make more aware choices, take more aware actions, and be more present with our thoughts as we work to create spirit-filled lives. Through our intentional behavior, we ask deeper questions of ourselves that help us bring out the best of who we are and help us develop greater connection to Spirit.

CONNECTING TO THE SPIRITUAL

Changing our thought and behavior habits is a lifelong endeavor. As we begin to make long overdue changes in our lives, we are sometimes tempted to think that the power to change comes solely from our own efforts. The following prayer suggestions will help you maintain an attitude of humility and keep God at the center of your life:

Prayer Suggestions

• Pray for help to remove any internal obstacles to living more intentionally.

• Pray for understanding of the true source of your dissatisfaction.

• Pray to receive the questions of greatest benefit to you now.

• Pray for the fortitude to take the necessary actions to change your situation.

• Pray in thanksgiving for the guidance and help you receive.

PERSONAL MEDITATION

Native American Story

An old Cherokee told his granddaughter about a fight between two wolves that goes on inside him. He said, "One wolf is evil: Anger, envy, sorrow, regret, greed, arrogance, self-pity, guilt, resentment, inferiority, lies, false pride, superiority and ego. The other wolf is good: Joy, peace, love, hope, serenity, humility, kindness, benevolence, empathy, generosity, truth, compassion and faith.

The granddaughter thought about it for a minute and then asked her grandfather, "Which wolf wins?"

The old Cherokee simply replied, "The one I feed."

This brief story underscores for me the importance of being awake, intentional and vigilant. Our automatic behavior thrives within us; how we feed it is by being asleep to its influence in our lives. To feed our intentional behavior we must learn to awaken to the yearnings within us that exist to pull us forward into being inspired contributors to humanity.

Meditate on this story to help you remember that something of value is always struggling within you to take shape.

When you are living on autopilot, you limit your full expression and experience of joy, peace, love, hope, serenity, humility, kindness, benevolence, empathy, generosity, truth, compassion and faith.

SERVING OTHERS
How to Be Available

In *The Power of Myth*, Joseph Campbell said that each of us is a completely unique creature and if we are ever to give any gift to the world, it will have to come out of our own experience and fulfillment of our own potentialities, not someone else's. Taking yourself off autopilot signals the start of your journey toward an authentic, spirit-filled life. Authenticity is the natural state of being that lies beyond our conditioning and limited beliefs; it is that state of being upon which truly creative and inspired lives are built.

The capacity to be authentic is shaped by spiritual connection, ongoing learning and transformation, and contribution. As you develop along your spiritual path, a natural desire to serve others may emerge. Evaluate your talents and skills; understand where your passions lie; and, determine where you can be of greatest service. Then, reach out. Sometimes we needn't go any further than to serve those closest to us.

Your spiritual development will be greatly enhanced by sharing with others your wisdom, who you are today and who you are becoming.

PUTTING IT ALL TOGETHER

Taking yourself off autopilot is a function of increased awareness and the behavior change that flows from that awareness. Changing our behavior is a function of embodying new patterns of habit. The practices we engage in daily shift our experience because they shift what we pay attention to.

You will need to exercise discipline to transform any practice into a habit. Following the steps below will help you develop the discipline to form new habits:

1. **Reinforce what you're trying to do** ---If you practice your habit-to-be at the same time and in the same place every day, you'll begin to do it automatically. You won't have to be prompted or reminded.

2. **Schedule it** --- Consciously incorporate your new practice into your daily schedule. Write it into your daily schedule as an appointment with yourself and **keep that appointment with yourself sacred**. Treat it like it's an appointment with the most important person in the world (because it is).

3. **Remember it** --- Write yourself a reminder. Write a note to yourself and tape it in key locations around your environment (home, office, car, etc.). This step is especially helpful for those prone to bouts of forgetfulness.

4. **Make an initial commitment of 21 days** --- It has been said that if you do the same thing the same way for twenty-one days in a row, you will turn that behavior into a habit. The secret is to do it every day, without missing a day. Don't let yourself off the hook. The objective is to maintain your momentum long enough for the new

behavior to maintain itself. Once your momentum can maintain itself, then you've developed a new habit.

5. **Ask for support** --- Don't be ashamed to ask for support. Sometimes having another person hold us accountable for keeping our word with ourselves is just the added support we need to "get us over the hump."

PART II

REINVENTING YOURSELF

Chapter Five

Eliminate Your Worst Enemy

PERSONAL REFLECTION

Sabotage is an interesting concept. The dictionary defines sabotage as "an act of malicious damage; deliberately poor workmanship, intended to cause damage; obstruction of plans, aims, etc. as in secret resistance."

Let's focus on the part of the definition that talks about obstruction of plans, aims, etc, as in secret resistance. Have you (as I have) declared yourself to be a wonderful starter, but not such a great finisher? I finally realized after many years of trying to figure out why I was living that statement that I was a victim of my own sabotage. I was restricting my own plans by saying that I did. What a revelation! I still struggle with that issue, but I don't let myself hear it or say it. I have changed my paradigm to say, "I am working to finish what I start, to follow through on my commitments, and to act on my good intentions."

LOOKING INWARD

There are other forms of self-sabotage, too, and some of them are subtle. Procrastination is one of the more obvious forms of self-sabotage. I have to be especially careful to stay within the positive kind of "when---then" statements. Here's a typical example of a negative when-then statement. "When I have all my bills paid, then I'll start a savings account." Uh-huh. Or…"when I lose the weight I need to lose, then I'll join a gym. I can't join now, because I don't look good in gym shorts." This kind of self-sabotage is sneaky, because you can't always tell you're doing it. At least I couldn't. Positive when-then statements are great. You get to choose the reward. "When I put \$\$\$ in my savings account for ___months in a row, then I'll reward myself by _____ (not taking out the money and blowing it!)" "When I work out at the gym for 3 months, then I'll reward myself by _____.

Not paying attention to what we need to do or ignoring our needs is another form of self -sabotage that has affected me. Doing what we know we should not do is the other side of this same coin. Most of my bad habits are a direct result of one of these two faults. Maybe you can relate to an example of mine that may help you. Let me take you back to the issue of needing to lose a few pounds. Not paying attention to my need to lose some weight doesn't make the weight go away. Eating a candy bar while standing at the kitchen sink is the other side of that coin. Other more dangerous behaviors fall into the same category. We don't always recognize them for what they are.

WISDOM FROM THE AGES

Folklore, children's stories, fable, myths, and stories that have a statement like, "…and the moral of the story is…" tell us much about self-sabotage. Procrastination, negative self-talk, and bad habits formed as a result of self-sabotage are often the reason why accidents, perils, and other awful things happen to the main character in the story. Sometimes there is a happy ending and sometimes there isn't. The next story illustrates this very clearly.

The Maiden, the Mountain, and the Serpent

It was a bitterly cold day when the young maiden was forced to make a trek to the top of the mountain. The path was clear, but there was snow and ice on both sides of the trail. She bundled herself into her heaviest robes and head covering, picked up the pack that she had to carry to the top of the mountain, and began her arduous journey.

Just as she approached the base of the trail that led upward, she was stopped by a voice that called to her. "Please help me. I too must go to the top of the mountain and I can't do it by myself in this weather." The maiden looked around, but the only living creature she could see was a great serpent lying coiled by the side of the path. Surely the serpent could not have spoken to her.

She was about to pass by the serpent when it raised its head and spoke to her again, begging to be carried to the top of the mountain. The maiden was frightened. The serpent was poisonous and even though it could barely move in the chill of the day, she was reluctant to provide the help it was asking for.

The serpent begged again and the maiden, out of the kindness of her heart, consented to carry it to the top. She picked it up and tucked it into her robes where it was warmed by the heat of her body. As they struggled upward, the serpent hissed encouragement to her, helping her to believe that she could do it.

They finally got to the top of the mountain and she was releasing the serpent from her robes. Suddenly it pierced her arm with its venomous fangs, forcing its poison deep within her system. As she lay dying, she asked the serpent why it had done this to her. The serpent responded, "You knew what I was when you picked me up."

KEY THOUGHTS

I remember how shocked I was the first time I heard this story and you may be asking yourself how a story like that made it into this book that is meant to be encouraging and uplifting. I included it to make a strong point. We poison ourselves every time we engage in any behavior that is self-destructive, sabotages our good intentions or interferes with our progress no matter what we're working on.

We've talked about three deadly forms of self-sabotage: self-talk, procrastination, and not taking care of our needs or doing what we know we shouldn't do. We've also talked about changing our self-talk and using the right kind of when-then statements. Now it's your turn. Notice what you consistently say about yourself. If it is negative or feels like you might be sabotaging yourself, try to change the paradigm. Here are some strategies to implement.

- Be vigilant about your self-talk. You will *"speak it into existence;"* whatever it is. Write down everything you say about yourself. Assess at the end of the day. When I was a little girl, my mom told me to ask myself these questions when I was talking about another person: Is it kind? Is it true? Is it necessary? These are not bad questions to consider when you are assessing your own self-talk.

- *When-then* statements can work for you or against you. You get to decide. Set up some when-then statements that reflect a personal goal that you have set.

- Procrastination takes away much of your ability to make proactive choices. Monitor your tendency to procrastinate. Reward yourself (maybe a great when-then statement) when you don't.

- Taking care of yourself includes not only doing what you know is good for you. It also involves not doing what you know is bad for you. Record your behaviors for a day, a week, or longer until you recognize patterns that are working for you or those that are working against you. Work to reward yourself in appropriate ways when you note positive changes. Keep it up. Behaviors don't form patterns over night. They don't disappear over night either.

CONNECTING TO THE SPIRITUAL

Is there a spiritual component to these exercises? I believe there is. Whatever we do to enhance our potential and fulfill our destiny is a spiritual activity. As we grow ever closer to understanding and applying our gifts and talents, we are becoming more of who we were meant to be. I don't believe that our purpose is to sabotage ourselves even in small ways. I am not implying that habits of negative self-talk and all the other forms of self sabotage that are discussed in this chapter are easy to change. Indeed, I think this requires the journey of a lifetime spent in reflection, refining, and reward. You first must believe that you are worthy of the effort it will take to develop your potential in all areas of your life.

We talk a lot about balance. Monitoring yourself through all the exercises mentioned here will help you determine if and where you might not be experiencing balance. You can work to correct it. I do want to caution you, however. A balanced life doesn't necessarily mean that every day is balanced. I think you'd drive yourself crazy trying to achieve that. Take a longer view of yourself. Do you feel that you experience balance over a week's time or over a month? Consider the long-range view in most of the work you do on yourself and you won't feel discouraged if you have a few bad moments.

Prayer Suggestions

- Pray for the discipline to only engage in positive self-talk.

- Pray for some great "when-then" statements that will make a difference in your life or in someone else's.

- Pray for the ability to stop any tendencies you have to procrastinate.

- Pray that you will be able to overcome the temptation to engage in self-destructive behavior of any kind.

- Pray that you will cease all forms of self-sabotage.

PERSONAL MEDITATION

What difference does it make if you engage in sabotage against yourself or against other people? It makes all the difference in the world. Sabotage by its very definition is destructive. As defined earlier it represents an act of malicious damage. Action like this is usually not random. It represents thought and a deliberate attempt to cause resistance or obstruction. Bad habits don't just happen. Someone told me once that forming a bad habit is hard work, can make you feel ill, and can cause the body to experience great stress. Soon, however, the habit takes over and doesn't seem so bad. But, it still is.

Changing habits and patterns of behavior is worth all the work it takes to undo the damage. Even years of damage can be reversed. So it is with changing habits of negative self-talk and other forms of sabotage. Once a new positive habit is firmly installed, it will prove to be as strong as the previous bad habit.

Understand that you are worth the effort to change all your paradigms for the better. Only when you give this gift to yourself are you able to effectively serve others.

SERVING OTHERS
How to Be Available

One of the best ways to serve others is simply to be available. Learn to listen with a willingness to just listen. Not everyone wants or needs a solution to his or her situation posed by anyone else. You may decide to intervene if someone else is engaging in statements of self-sabotage. Intervention is risky, but perhaps the other person in this scenario is unaware of his or her own self-talk. Be sensitive to the efforts you have put into your own transition from self-sabotage to positive affirmations and recognize that it is not easy for anyone to accomplish.

Above all, work to avoid sabotaging someone else's efforts to change for the better. All the exercises you've completed won't help your friend if you engage with them in any sort of sabotage. You may need to simply ask your friend to define your role in the situation they are working on. Honor what your friend requests of you. You may be itching to offer advice or tell your own story, but resist the temptation. Your relationship will be the stronger for it.

PUTTING IT ALL TOGETHER

Why is it so difficult to form positive habits, so easy to break them, and so easy to form negative habits? I don't know and I wish I did. I do know that it takes constant vigilance for me to stay "on the straight and narrow" when it comes to the goals I've set and the habits I want to cultivate.

Maybe we're made with the desire to succumb to various forms of self-sabotage. Maybe the statement "steel sharpens steel" applies as much to us as it does to honing a knife blade. I remember a high school friend of mine whose mother was dying of cancer. I expressed sorrow and sympathy for her struggle and my friend said that her mother felt like she was a gemstone in the tumbler of life. Her struggle represented what happens in a stone tumbler when all the rough places are made smooth and beautiful.

That powerful image has stayed with me for over forty years and I take comfort in it. The battles we face every day may or may not severely test us and test our faith. They do make us stronger, more resilient, and better able to deal with all the guises and disguises that sabotage throws our way. Be strong, be resolute, be confident in your ability to become a better person every day.

Chapter Six

Shatter the Myths That You Live By

PERSONAL REFLECTION

When I was a little girl, I was very impressionable, as are most children. Some of the information that I absorbed as truth was good for me and some of it wasn't. I was almost an adult before I could correctly process statements like "You're dumb" and "You're ugly." These statements started innocently enough, as do most insults traded by siblings, cousins, and other "childhood terrorists". One of the most difficult lessons for me, and one of the most valuable, was not to allow myself to say such mean things to myself.

As I became aware of the potential power of positive self-talk, I was stunned to realize the potential power of negative self-talk. Coupled with the realization of that power was the realization that the absorption of comments from others was a significant force in my life as well. How was I to absorb only the positive comments, the ones that would help me to develop my potential? Further, how was I going to learn to filter out the unwanted and unwarranted comments? The answers to these questions have become a sustaining process in my life. Every day I am learning better methods for coping with all kinds of messages, both the ones I receive and the ones I deliver to myself.

LOOKING INWARD

Self-talk is an incredibly powerful force, one that we don't always recognize for what it is. Negative self-talk is the source of four of the most powerful and pervasive myths in our culture. These myths have been present and affecting us practically since the dawn of time. Some women are so inculcated with these particular myths that they would swear they are true. Such is the power.

Myth #1: *My needs should come last, after my family, my home, my work, my community, my volunteer efforts, my church or synagogue, my friends, my..., my..., my...etc.*

This is a self-perpetuating myth if there ever was one. After all of that, there is simply no time for self. Sometimes we pride ourselves as being SuperMom, SuperWorker, SuperSpouse, and so on when the reality is we just need to reassess and reorder our priorities. I am not suggesting that you abandon what you are doing and forget about the importance of your to-do list. I am merely saying put yourself on the list.

Myth #2: *The direction for my life should come from outside myself. I need to be guided to find my true calling.*

Again, if we allow ourselves to believe this myth, it, too, becomes self-perpetuating. When we are children the direction for our lives comes from our caregivers, teachers and others who provide the guidance we require. As adults, however, we need to establish ourselves as the person in charge of who we are and who we are becoming. This is not always a smooth transition and not always a steady forward progression. There may still be areas in which we do expect and need outside influences to guide and direct us. We should at least be open to suggestion. The important concept here is to raise our awareness of self.

Myth #3: *It is required of us to measure up to certain standards of appearance and performance.*

Whose standards? What kind of appearance? What level of performance? I worked with one supervisor whose mantra was "Does it pass the test of 'good enough?'" I didn't particularly like that statement at the time and I still don't. It seems to me that good is the enemy of great. It does, however, point out that again we should strive for the ability to assess our own appearance and performance, continue to work for growth, continue to work for improvement, continue to work for development.

The media is, in my opinion, largely responsible for the false impressions that we tend to accept. You probably know the ones I mean: This product will give you perfect skin, the perfect figure, the perfect meal for your family's health, the perfect vacation, the perfect home, the perfect relationship, the perfect spouse, the perfect career, and so on and so on. Does anyone really believe all that? Apparently some do. Do you?

Myth #4:   *I am not worthy.*

This is the most dangerous myth of all. I was speaking recently with a dear friend who said that in high school he was on the track team for the mile race. During one practice the team was running together around the track and my friend realized that no one on his team was anywhere close to catching him. He felt wonderful! In the locker room later, a teammate remarked that my friend's performance meant nothing, that he was much faster, and so on. The result of that idle remark had so much impact on my friend that he never won another race. As an adult, he looks back on that incident with regret. As Eleanor Roosevelt said **no one can make you feel inferior without your consent.** Don't give it! Don't give your consent to "well-meaning friends" who criticize, complain, whine, or in any other way cause you to feel that you are not worthy.

WISDOM FROM THE AGES

The Myth of Sisyphus

Sisyphus was a mythical king of Corinth. His name means "very wise" or "shrewd" in Greek, and he was certainly that …at least in the short run.

Sisyphus angered Zeus when he spread the word that Zeus slept with the nymph Aegina. Sisyphus had seen a larger-than-life mighty eagle, Zeus's bird, carry her off to an island, and told her river-god father when he came by looking for her.

Zeus easily drove the angry father away with his thunderbolt, but for spilling the beans, Zeus ordered his brother Hades to seize Sisyphus and take him to Tartarus, where men are punished for their evil deeds. Sisyphus, however, used his wiles to turn the tables on the god and made Hades a prisoner on earth. With Death in chains, no one, not even those mortally injured on the battlefield, could die. This was totally unacceptable to the war god, Ares, and he took it upon himself to personally set Hades free and hand him Sisyphus.

However, Sisyphus had another trick up his sleeve. Before descending to Tartarus, he instructed his wife to do nothing with his body. Once in the Underworld he approached Persephone, the Queen of the Underworld, and asked her to let him return to earth to arrange for his burial, so his soul could find rest. She agreed, believing his promise to return in three days. Once he was back on earth, however, Sisyphus refused to return. This time the god Hermes was the one to bring him back by force.

Sisyphus was stuck. Because he had caused Zeus and the other gods so much trouble, he was given an especially frustrating punishment. He was condemned to roll a huge block of stone up a hill for all eternity. Each time Sisyphus rolled or pushed the stone to the top of the hill, the massive stone rolled back down to the bottom of the hill, where he had to get it and start pushing all over again.

KEY THOUGHTS

A Sisyphean labor means a task that is never complete, one in which you can make no progress, one that leaves you tired and confused.

Think about the self-perpetuating myths that are mentioned earlier in this chapter. If you examine them objectively, you will see that they have the same characteristics of the myth about Sisyphus. Perhaps you have unconsciously taken on the role of Sisyphus. The more you labor under falsehoods like these myths and others, the larger your stone becomes and the more frustrating it is to try to push it up the hill.

We all know the fairy tales that featured a "good mother", usually a queen or someone with a lot of authority. These same stories usually also featured a "bad mother", often a witch or some scary character that might actually eat the children. There is a common thread in tales like these. Have you noticed that the good mother is usually dead, busy, or missing? The bad mother figure is the one that relates to the children, even if she is busy trying to "fatten them up." What are we to learn from these examples? Is the present, nurturing, encouraging good mother the stuff of fairy tales yet to be written? Is the whole myth of impossibly high standards truly a myth? How do we know when the standards we have set are impossibly high?

Sometimes it takes an objective conversation with someone you trust who can guide you to discover that you are indeed responding to the various myths that are mentioned in this chapter. You may indeed have myths of your own that are impacting you in negative or unhealthy ways.

Sometimes girls and young women in our society are caught up in these myths, accept them as truth, and fail to live up to their potential. Perhaps you have been caught up in these myths yourself. Do you believe you "can do it all?" What does that mean to you? Do you suspect that somehow you are not "worthy?" What does that mean? How does that myth affect your reality? These are questions worth pondering.

CONNECTING TO THE SPIRITUAL

You may be wondering how your involvement in the myths that are mentioned here, and/or your awareness of the involvement of someone you care about can possibly have a spiritual overtone. The spark of desire for excellence and achievement is divinely inspired. In a positive sense, we are drawn to people who encourage us to be all that we can be. In contrast, we may also be drawn to people who discourage us, who don't value us an individuals, and who perhaps feed the myth that we (not they) should be able to do it all, that guidance for our lives should come from outside ourselves (from them, in some cases) and that we are not worthy.

Prayer Suggestions

- Pray for the wisdom to recognize any myth that may be controlling you.

- Pray for the strength to search for the truth behind the myth.

- Pray in gratitude for the willingness to change.

- Pray for the courage to face the consequences of the changes you are willing to make.

PERSONAL MEDITATION

As you pray, you are open to the spirit-inspired subconscious thoughts that connect you to your real self, and indeed, to others. Think about the times that you have been troubled by a crisis of some kind either for yourself or for someone you love. Perhaps you have experienced, as I have, a spontaneous sense of relief, of solution, or of practical suggestions that seem to come from nowhere.

Napoleon Hill, a significant author of the late 19th century, believed that we are connected by an all-powerful mind. If we tune into that power, we benefit from the thoughts and experiences of others. I've also heard it stated that we are "a resurrection people". That means that no matter what happens to us, that we almost always have the inner strength to bounce back in about three days. I don't know if I believe in the three days theory as it applies to a crisis in our lives, but it's an interesting thought.

I think we can apply these two ideas to the attempts we make to overcome the myths. After we pray for the insight to recognize myths for what they are and for the strength to replace them with truth, it takes an openness to listen to our inner voice and some time to live with the new truth. Give yourself permission to take these steps.

- Stop for a moment and calm your thoughts. Let go of your anxieties and look around.
- What do you see? You see a world filled with beauty; you see a life filled with possibilities; you see dreams being born, being nurtured and being fulfilled.
- Yes, there are challenges. But more than these, there is love; there is goodness; there is joy. The future is uncertain. That means there are no limits.
- You may have wandered away from yourself. Now is the time to come back.

SERVING OTHERS
How to Be Available

Being available is a mindset more than it is a function of time. We've heard the concept of "quality time". I believe that term refers to any relationship in which we invest ourselves. Active listening, accepting and learning comprise a four-step process.

1. The first step is merely to serve as witness - being present and aware of the meaning of the words being spoken and the meaning behind the words. Ask for clarification if you need it.

2. The second step in this kind of listening process is acknowledgment. Statements to the speaker might include, " I know this is tough; it's hard to know what to do". Notice that no advice is given.

3. The third step is to determine the feelings being expressed. Again, you may need to ask.. "Are you feeling overwhelmed, sad, determined, etc?"

4. The fourth step involves "asking" as well. This time your job as the listener is to ask what the speaker desires. "What do you want? What would you like?" Notice that the question is not "What do you want me to do?"

Many times when you are involved in this kind of conversation, it is tempting to try to "fix" the problem. That's not your job. Your job is to listen, to affirm, to encourage, and to be available. If you are asked for a solution, work through the steps listed above again.

PUTTING IT ALL TOGETHER

The purpose of this chapter is to assist you in recognizing myths that are interfering with your ability to perform at your best, to feel confident about being in control of your choices, and to allow positive changes in your relationships.

It may be very helpful to review your thoughts from the journal entries or exercises that you recorded earlier. It takes time and work to recognize the myths for what they are. "We've always done it that way" and "We've never done it that way" are two of the mind-numbing myths or excuses that will prevent change and growth.

Try to avoid that kind of self-talk and remain open to sudden insight that will lead you down a more positive path of self-talk. The process is challenging, frustrating at times, but most of all it is rewarding.

Continue to work. Continue to be open to Spirit. Continue to reward yourself for positive changes, and continue to grow.

Cherish the person that you are and the person that you are becoming.

Chapter Seven

Cultivate Your Positive Thought Power

PERSONAL REFLECTION

Thirteen years ago I was in a career I enjoyed, doing work that was both challenging and intrinsically rewarding. The only problem, however, was that I felt undervalued for my contributions, skills and knowledge, unappreciated and <u>definitely</u> underpaid in my job.

When I grasped after some time that my whining and complaining weren't going to change the situation, I decided to look for a new job. As I started dreaming about where I would seek future employment, I figured that since I was dreaming I might as well dream big. That's when I made the decision to change careers completely!

In the dreaming process, I focused on defining a career for myself that would allow me to do work about which I was passionate and for which I was uniquely suited. Once I had my ideal career and position in mind, I wrote down my vision of what I wanted, along with the salary I desired. In reviewing what I had written, I recognized immediately that my vision seemed more like a pipedream or an item on a wish list, rather than a reality I could actually materialize.

I realized, then, that the likelihood of achieving my goal was very slim because my sense of possibility was limited. I went to work to change my attitude and to enlarge my view of what was possible. The main area of focus for my internal transformation was in the area of money. At that time in my life I was only earning $26,000 a year, which I felt was very modest for my responsibilities and the work I performed.

I was grateful for interesting work and felt blessed to be working. At the same time, however, I felt that my salary represented, not so much my value to the company, but what within myself I felt was my true worth as a human being. Logically, I knew that my thinking was erroneous, but when I examined the results being manifested in my life, I knew that issues of self-worth and deservedness were operating at the emotional level.

To perform a radical overhaul of my attitude, I had to shift my perception that the company was "out to get me." I decided that even if the company did not recognize my accomplishments, I still had to continue to work diligently in carrying out my job. I also needed to bring to work a more optimistic spirit by emphasizing and keeping my attention on the positive aspects of my life and my job. These actions helped me relate to my circumstances in a much more effective way.

More difficult to alter was my relationship with money, which became a metaphor for my relationship with myself. For this transformation, I had to work actively to replace my thoughts and feeling of low self-worth with more self-empowering thoughts. I also stopped speaking about lack and began speaking about abundance, thereby creating an inner feeling of expansion and an internal expectancy that blessings would flow into my life.

Changing my perspective and transforming my relationship with myself required vigilant and intentional work. I constantly monitored my thoughts and feelings, worked with affirmations and released the outcomes to God. Within a year, I achieved a goal I never thought possible before I began my journey of transformation. I changed my career to one that I love and still benefit from today. The first year in my new job, I earned two and a half times my previous salary and worked my way up to a six-figure salary within five years!

I have experienced for myself, and wholeheartedly agree with, the wisdom of William James, an early twentieth century thought leader and essayist, when he said, "The greatest discovery of my generation is that a human being can alter his life by altering his attitudes of mind."

LOOKING INWARD

A vibrant, fulfilling life where we are in touch with Spirit cannot be experienced through a veil of negativity, limitedness and pessimism. Spirit-filled living absorbs our view and helps us see the world through eyes of awe and wonderment, unclouded by the sense of lack, doubt and distrust.

While pessimism is typically thought of as negative thinking, it also manifests as limited thinking, as shown in the chart below.

Negative Thinking	Limited Thinking
Seeing the Glass as Half Empty – Looking at what's missing rather than what's present	**Perfectionist Thinking** – Thinking you have to perform perfectly but feeling you consistently fall short of your own high standards
Being Hypercritical – Tendency to look for and point out what's wrong	**"No Choice" Thinking** – Thinking that you have no choice other than to tolerate that which is disagreeable to you
Being Hyper-Vigilant for Danger – Tendency to expect problems to arise	**Limited Possibility Thinking** –Settling for small dreams because of issues of worthiness, buying into a limited view of what's possible espoused by others.

Seeing the Glass as Half Empty – Looking at what's missing rather than at what's present

As the story goes, people will either see a glass partially filled with liquid as half full or half-empty. Half-empty people evaluate situations through a lens that shows them a world that is lacking. Their attention is fixated on how a situation falls short from some ideal picture they have in their mind. Half-full people recognize the blessings in their lives and feel a deep sense of gratitude for what they have been given.

Being Hypercritical – Tendency to look for and point out what's wrong

People who are hypercritical seem to relentlessly criticize everyone and everything around them. Being analytical and having a "critical eye" are strengths some people possess which help them operate in methodical ways. As strengths, both being analytical and having a critical eye are very useful for the systematic investigation and diagnosis of problems. However, being hypercritical is a strength overused to the point of developing into a weakness. People who are hypercritical have an orientation to life that results in their constant faultfinding of others and a focus on what's wrong in their environment.

Being Hyper-Vigilant for Danger – Tendency to expect problems to arise

People who are hyper-vigilant for danger are generally never satisfied with their positive circumstances or their accomplishments. These people are unable to relax with the goodness they receive. They feel an internal sense of anxiety that causes them to be constantly on the lookout for the crisis that's going to take away their blessings, knock them off center and destroy their sense of happiness.

Perfectionist Thinking – Thinking you have to perform perfectly but feeling you consistently fail to live up to your own high standards

Perfectionist thinking is a variation of being hypercritical. In this case, the focus of attention is on the thinker. These people are possessed by a harsh inner critic that drives them to achieve perfection, but rarely allows them to experience success or satisfaction with what they accomplish.

"No Choice" Thinking – Thinking that you have no choice other than to tolerate that which is disagreeable to you

People who think they have no choices in certain situations feel boxed in by the circumstances in their life. Sometimes seeing that we have no choice in the matter of our lives means that we fear taking the necessary risks to change our situation. At other times, it means that, for whatever reason, we want to hold on to the way things are. While we cannot always change our circumstances, we can change how we relate to those circumstances.

Limited Possibility Thinking – Having small dreams, settling for less because of issues of worthiness, buying into a limited view of what's possible espoused by others

My story at the beginning of this chapter is a prime example of limited possibility thinking. In my case, as I grew, I became aware of a big dream I wanted to accomplish, but recognized that my thinking would hinder my progress. In order to overcome feelings of unworthiness that were blocking me and limiting my chances of success, I had to alter my thinking by retraining my mind.

Pessimism is an habitual thought pattern and a learned response. People are pessimistic because they have learned to consistently choose to interpret the events around them in a negative light. But, just as pessimism is a learned habitual response, so it can be unlearned.

Many factors contribute to negativity, among them are:

- Powerlessness which stems from people being resigned about their ability to change their circumstances
- Fear of taking the necessary risks to grow or change
- Subconscious attempts to protect oneself from future disappointments (real or perceived)
- Influences on our thinking gained through family or social experiences

- Inherited conversations from our most important caregivers and others we respect
- Hopelessness caused by clinical depression (which is outside the scope of this book)

Examine your own life.

- Where do you harbor negative thoughts or a sense of pessimism?
- How has that affected your actions?

WISDOM FROM THE AGES

The Donkey in the Well

One day a farmer's donkey fell into a deep well. The animal cried pitifully for hours as the farmer tried to figure out what to do. Finally the farmer made a decision: The animal was old, and the well needed to be filled in anyway. It just wasn't worth trying to retrieve the donkey.

He invited all his neighbors to come over and help him. They all grabbed a shovel and began to shovel dirt into the well. At first, the donkey realized what was happening and cried horribly.

Then, to everyone's amazement, he quieted down. A few shovel loads later, the farmer finally looked down the well. He was astonished at what he saw. With each shovel of dirt that hit his back, the donkey was doing something amazing. He would shake it off and take a step up.

As the farmer's neighbors continued to shovel dirt on top of the animal, he would shake it off and take a step up. Pretty soon, everyone was amazed as the donkey stepped up over the edge of the well and happily trotted off!

Life is going to shovel dirt on you, all kinds of dirt. The trick to getting out of the well is to shake it off and take

> a step up. Each of our troubles is a stepping-stone. We can get out of the deepest wells just by not stopping, never giving up! Shake it off and take a step up.

Over-excitement, panic and operating as if our situation is hopeless all hinder our ability to be resourceful. Likewise, expecting that life will never throw dirt in our faces sets us up to be powerless and defeated in the face of unforeseen events.

Our capacity to maintain a feeling of positive expectancy that favorable outcomes will ensue in the long term – regardless of how situations present themselves to us in the short term – will help us become optimistic thinkers.

KEY THOUGHTS

A growing amount of research has shown that a pessimistic outlook will invariably not only take a toll on your career, but on your health as well. Pessimists are not good at handling stress. They have less confidence and are not as well equipped with effective coping methods. Therefore, looking at the circumstances in your life negatively will not only stress you out, but also will tax your immune system and lead to health problems and more negativity. All in all, a bit of a vicious circle …

> *Your attitude acts as a filtering lens that colors the way you see events, circumstances, the people around you, and even yourself. For example, if the lens you're wearing is blue, everything around you appears blue. If the lens is red, everything around you appears red. Likewise, if the lens you're wearing is negative and pessimistic, everything around you will have a negative tint.*

Negative thinking is a habit that can be transformed like any habit if you apply the necessary discipline. First, you need to recognize the extent to which pessimism has negatively affected the quality of your life and hindered your ability to attract to you the circumstances, people and opportunities you desire. Next, you need to determine the steps you will take to change your negative or limited view of life.

If you tend to look at life through a lens of negativity, the following ideas when practiced consistently will change your attitude, your disposition and your circumstances:

1. ***Take a creative accounting of your life.*** Stop focusing on what's wrong in your life or what's missing from your life and start keeping a mental checklist of all the good things that happen to you. Simply focusing on the positive can really boost your mood. It has been said that we become what we pay attention to. To make the positives more tangible, write them down on a daily basis.

2. ***Avoid comparisons.*** Stop comparing yourself to others. There will always be someone smarter, wealthier or more accomplished than you, but making comparisons will not help you have a positive attitude about yourself. Forget about them, and concentrate on yourself and what you can do to change your circumstances. If you must make comparisons, compare yourself today with where you were in your life a year or two (or more) ago. In all likelihood, you have made more progress than you think!

3. ***Pay attention to how your mood affects your outlook.*** If you are in good spirits, your day-to-day experiences and interactions will be more positive. Don't wallow in muddy negativity – work on accepting any bad news or experiences; learn from them and move forward.

4. ***Dismiss putdowns.*** Nothing others say can ever change your own intrinsic worth as a person. Putdowns will only lead to insecurity if you let them. If you find that you continually suffer putdowns from the same people, either let them know their remarks hurt your feelings, spend less time with them or remove them from your life, if appropriate.

5. ***Surround yourself with positive, supportive women.*** It is very difficult to maintain a negative attitude when you place yourself in the company of people you enjoy who are positive and supportive. An important study done in the late 1990s found that genuine friendships between women counteract

the stress many women feel on a daily basis. Decreasing the stress in your life will help you to adopt a more relaxed, effective approach to problems and improve the negativity and sense of futility you may feel.

6. ***Laugh – loudly and often.*** No doubt, you have heard the story of Dr. Norman Cousins. Norman Cousins, diagnosed with a disease characterized as fatal, healed himself by watching old comedy films and putting himself on a prescription of high daily dosages of Vitamin C and laughter. In addition to raising one's spirits, a good laugh has also been shown to decrease stress.

7. ***Don't punish yourself for being human.*** Sometimes, despite all your actions and good intentions, you may still find yourself harboring a negative attitude about your circumstances. In these cases, acknowledge the truth to yourself, chock it up to "having an off day" and nurture yourself instead – even if you don't feel like it. Recent research has shown that there are indeed times when women need to "retreat into their caves" to regroup and renew themselves.

CONNECTING TO THE SPIRITUAL

The Law of Attraction states that our thoughts, magnetized by our feelings, become a force that draws to us positive or negative experiences. In applying the Law of Attraction, we are required to do more than just think positively. Our positive thoughts must be accompanied by deep feelings of joy, love, and abundance.

As we practice the Law of Attraction, there is no better way to generate positive feelings than by focusing on God and the blessings God has brought into our lives. All gifts we receive flow from Spirit and we must never lose sight of the fact that God is in control of all our circumstances.

As we cultivate our positive thought power, it is important to attend to the nourishing of our spirit by taking the following specific intentional actions:

Acknowledge your Accomplishments – Even the Small Ones

Each thing you do well, however small, is an accomplishment, even if it is a routine task. You'll feel more in control of your circumstances if you see tasks as achievements and, as a result, you'll feel more in control of your life. Hopefully, people will notice how well you do things and just how valuable you are. Even if they don't, you will feel a sense of satisfaction from doing the task well.

Celebrate Your Wins.

It is important that you don't take yourself and your accomplishments for granted. By recognizing important personal victories and accepting things you do well, you will increase your sense of self-appreciation and elevate your mood tremendously.

Maintain a Gratitude Journal

Recording the things for which you are grateful on a daily basis does not have to take great effort and the return on your investment of time is enormous. To make this task easy, review your day and record the three things for which you are most grateful. As you pray, always remember to thank God earnestly for your circumstances. If you do this every day with sincerity and a certain amount of introspection and depth, you will find that the positive effects are cumulative.

Retrain Your Thoughts

Retraining your thoughts can be as simple as establishing a discipline to work on affirmations. But it is also possible that you will need counseling or coaching to help you examine some of your underlying perceptions. Don't be afraid to do what it takes to turn your thinking around. Your life will become richer as a result.

PERSONAL MEDITATION

As you enter into your time of prayer and reflection, think about the changes that have occurred in your life over the past year:

- How have you grown?
- How have your circumstances changed for the better?

- What have you learned from your failures?
- In what ways have you grown wiser?
- What have you gained?
- What difficulties have you triumphed over?

In addition to the questions above, take time to pose and reflect on your own questions to help you fill your spirit with thanksgiving and gratitude. Rest in the experience of awe and wonder at how blessed you are. You may even wish to record your thoughts so you can review them during the times you are feeling down and to enable you to see the positive progression of your life over time.

If you engage in this kind of thoughtful reflection on a regular basis as part of your spiritual development program, you will reshape your thinking and your life.

SERVING OTHERS
How to Be Available

We often think that being positive and upbeat means putting on an enthusiastic and exuberant demeanor and dealing with problems in an optimistically blind manner. Quite the contrary, positive thought power doesn't overwhelm those around us with frenetic energy. It is an internal power that emanates from within us as a centered, peaceful, sensitive and calm strength.

Positive, centered energy is a contagious force. It uplifts the downtrodden, endows you with profound wisdom and demonstrates the power of God actively working in your life. As others come to you feeling stressed from the challenges of their lives, you can be a positive, supportive harbor of strength and serenity.

PUTTING IT ALL TOGETHER

We have a choice about how we see the world. We can we see the world as a hostile place that requires us to look for hidden signs of danger where there are none, or we can see it as welcoming place that offers many opportunities to allow peace and abundance to flow into our lives.

Cultivating our positive thought power demands a collaborative partnership with God. There is often a temptation to think that our material, emotional and spiritual gains come to us solely as a result of the work we do in garnering them. Whatever blessings accrue to us in our lives come as gifts from God, regardless of the personal effort we expend to accomplish our goals.

Positive thought power is more than simply thinking positively. It also requires that we authentically feel and acknowledge the power of love, joy and abundance in our lives, and that we allow ourselves to be touched by our deep and abiding gratitude for all we have been given.

PART III

Replacing Outmoded Habits with New Practices and Disciplines

Chapter Eight

Move Yourself from Dreams to Goals

PERSONAL REFLECTION

Contrary to many folks, I have always loved change. It didn't really matter what the change entailed as long as it was an opportunity for new beginnings. I loved to start new hobbies, start new ways of doing things around the house, change routines, start new self-improvement plans, etc. You name it and I would start "doing" it. My problem was I had a hard time making myself finish anything. That wasn't the fun part…starting was the fun part. I had lots of evidence to prove that I was operating this way. Maybe you can relate to some of my "starts". Several partially finished garments hung in my closet, some of them only needing a hem or some buttonholes or some other small finishing detail. Several partially finished crochet items were a silent testimony to starting and not finishing. Cross stitch projects, diaries, journals, even a dug out but not finished pond in my garden all served as reminders that I was on to something else. The thing is, I deluded myself into being convinced that I would finish everything "someday". I even described myself as "a wonderful starter…not such a hot finisher". And, we all realize that however you describe yourself you will become that person. Your subconscious will work overtime to make what you say about yourself come true. That's why your self-talk is so critical. I knew all that; in fact, I even taught that philosophy. However, I lived by the other famous philosophy "do as I say, not as I do". I operated that way throughout my adolescence and for several decades of my adult life. How did I break what was becoming a bad habit?

I changed my outlook regarding beginning and finishing from a chance remark made by my oldest daughter. We often visited over coffee at our house or their house, while the children were napping. This conversation had been the usual sharing time. I remarked about a project that she had finished recently, told her I admired her, and mentioned again, "I am such a great starter, and such a lousy finisher". She said, "Mom, it's only because you have heard yourself saying that for thirty years or so. " What she didn't realize was that her memories only went back about thirty years! I had probably been saying that for close to forty years, or even longer. Somehow that chance comment was a tremendous turning point for me.

I still love change. I still am very energized by beginning something new. However, I now understand the power of completion, and I'm proud to say that I now focus on the result as much as the process of organizing and beginning. What changed me? I learned to hold myself accountable by making lists. It seems like such a simple notion, but it was key for me. I make a list every day of at least ten things I intend to accomplish. A list of ten things is just right for me, because I have ten "starts" every day. You can be sure I check each one off as I do it. Some of the items on my daily list are stated in time blocks, such as "write for 15 minutes". That way I can fulfill the item on the list without the extra burden of having to finish a chapter, for example. You can also be sure that if I actually do something that wasn't on my original list I put it on there so I can have the satisfaction of checking it off.

LOOKING INWARD

New Year's resolutions…dreams…a wish list…goals. How are these concepts the same and, more importantly, how are they different? As you work through this chapter, you will learn the key components of the process of setting goals. By doing so, you will learn why New Year's resolutions, dreams, and your wish list don't always come to fruition. Almost everyone makes some kind of New Year's resolution, even if it's just an office joke. Almost everyone will admit to having dreams, even though they may not expect them to come true. Almost everyone has a wish list somewhere, even if it's just in his or her mind. Why do we take these concepts so lightly? I think it's because we don't have a systematic way of recording what we want to accomplish, how we will measure our progress, and how we will reward ourselves when we have done what we set out to do.

There is a SMART way to set goals. Many people are familiar with this goal-setting acronym, which stands for Specific, Measurable, Achievable, Reasonable, Time Bound. I think there is a SMART-ER way to set goals. Let's add Energizing and Rewarded to the system. First, however, let me show you why I think that you must know how to set goals to achieve your desires. Here is a typical New Year's Resolution: *I am going to lose weight.* Here is a typical dream: *I would love to be slim.* Here is a typical item on a wish list: *I wish I were wearing a smaller size, felt better and had more energy.* None of those statements is specific as to what, how, and when you are going to achieve what you want to do.

Here is the same idea expressed in a goal-oriented format: I am going to lose 1 pound a week for 12 weeks, starting the first of next month. Can you see the difference? It is Specific as to outcome. It is certainly Measurable. It is Achievable and Reasonable. It is Time bound. What's missing? The ER statements! We can energize the goal by telling a friend that we are working on this goal and ask that person to help us be accountable. We can use positive affirmations on a daily basis for auto-encouragement and we can talk about what we are moving toward...a slimmer, healthier self...rather than what we're moving away from...no ice cream, etc. for a while. It's important here to recognize that you only have to watch what you eat and how much you exercise **today.** Of course you have to do that every day, but it's easier to manage one day at a time.

What about the reward? That's up to you, but it should be something that you will deny yourself until you achieve the goal. It might be new shoes, a movie, a day trip or a longer one, or anything that pleases you. The reward should not cancel out the efforts you have made to achieve the goal. For example, this goal is about feeling healthier and being slimmer. A reward focused on food would not be a good idea until a period of maintenance is established.

In another scenario, let's talk about a goal related to your financial health. Suppose for a moment that your dream is to have no credit card debt, a healthy savings and/or investment program, and money for the causes you support. Resolution, dream, wish list item, or goal? How can this scenario be expressed as a goal? I believe that it represents a series of goals that can be overlapping, worked on at the same time, or worked on consecutively. How? Let's see.

In order for you to know how to resolve a credit card debt problem, you must know how you are using your money now. Get in the habit of writing down every cent you spend. Dedicate a notebook for this purpose. Keep it with you in your vehicle. Write down **everything,** even parking and other minor items. At this point you are just observing, not judging, what your spending habits are. After a month or two, analyze what you have been doing. Do you see areas of unnecessary expense? I don't know anyone who can't find some. It is now time to write the first goal related to this cash outflow.

Here's an example:

Specific: I will eliminate (dollar amount or percent) of my recorded expenses next month.

Measurable: Track the next month and see if you did it.

Achievable: You can do this with some thought and without feeling deprived.

Reasonable: If the dollar amount or percentage seems unreasonable, do it anyway this month and then adjust if you have to for next month. You may find that you're used to it by next month and you won't need to adjust.

Time Bound:	We're only talking about a month here, but you might have to adjust that, too, to a week or whatever.
Energizing:	Are you kidding? You will feel so empowered that you will be excited to do even more. Be careful...don't deny yourself too much, or the whole process will cause you to burn out.
Rewarded:	Be careful here, too. Don't set a reward that involves spending the money you saved. That will defeat your entire purpose for the exercise. Instead, reward yourself by paying what you saved as an extra payment toward a high interest credit card or by putting the money in a savings account.

The next goal should follow the same SMARTER pattern. Here's another example:

Specific: I will trim <u>(dollar amount or percent)</u> of my budget for food. Here is an area where you can save a considerable amount of money. If you currently spend money for a fast food meal several times a month, cut back one or two of those expenditures. How? Eat in...it's that simple. If it's a work-related expense, substitute with a meal carried from home. If it's a meal carried home from take out, you would do better by stopping off at the grocery store.

After you work through the whole SMARTER pattern, stop for a benchmark check and assessment. If you keep doing what you've been doing...trimming your recorded expenses and trimming your food expenditures...will you be getting ahead? Will you feel empowered? Will you be in control? I believe the feeling of control and empowerment will serve to energize you and will be its own reward.

Exercise

Think of the various areas of your life in broad categories. The categories I chose for myself included work, health and fitness, relationships, financial security, spiritual health, serving others, personal growth, and recreation. I allowed a whole page in my journal for each category. Under each broad category I listed everything I wanted and everything I hoped to accomplish. This activity took a long time and is still open-ended. I add items to various categories quite frequently. It's pleasurable to look back over the accomplishments I've made as well. You can do as I did and record the date of entry and the date of completion if you wish.

WISDOM FROM THE AGES

The Power of Faith

You must have faith in yourself to succeed, even if you have written worthy goals, have figured out how to make them "SMART-ER", and have an accountability buddy to help you stay on track. If you don't believe you are worthy of success, you won't be able to work on your goals without some sort of self-sabotage. The wisdom literature of Christianity declares in the book of Hebrews, chapter 11, "without faith it is impossible to please God." You can't please yourself either. Again in Hebrews, chapter 11 is the definition of faith: "Faith is the substance of things hoped for and the evidence of things not seen."

That is the perfect analogy to the way you should behave during the goal-setting process and during the successful completion of the goals. I have found that if I behave in the way that I have declared for myself I am much more likely to follow my own guidelines. Put in contemporary terms, this is an example of a paradigm shift. However, faith is not enough. In the Christian New Testament, the book of James declares in chapter 2, "Faith without works is dead." You can find example after example of statements like these throughout recorded history. If it were not so, would there be so much evidence? Use the wisdom of the ages to believe in yourself and what you can accomplish.

KEY THOUGHTS

I believe that my experience proves the theory I've been talking about. I faced the issue of an unhealthy lifestyle, with excessive weight, low energy, etc. I followed the SMARTER pattern to lose weight and it worked for me. Notice that I'm not telling you how to lose the weight. There are wonderful, slow paced, healthy ways to lose weight. Get some good advice from a health professional and follow it.

My husband and I also followed the SMARTER pattern to get ahead financially and it worked for us. It took quite a while, but so did getting into the poor financial habits in the first place. You can win your battles using this pattern of goal setting, too.

Think about the various areas in your life in which you feel that you don't have the control you want. You may feel overwhelmed if you try to tackle every area at the same time. It's not a bad idea, however, to write down all the things you'd like to work on or change. Once you have your list, you can prioritize the goals. Apply the SMART-ER system to the first change you want to make. You will probably discover, as I did, that when you understand the process, you will be able to work on more than one of your goals at the same time. That was perfect for someone as impatient as I was. There is another school of thought, however.

That is FOCUS...Follow One Course Until Successful. You'll have to be the judge as to how much you can handle without losing sight of your goal and where you are in the SMART-ER process. Whether you work on one goal at a time or choose to work in overlapping areas, there is one more step that will prove to be vitally important. Write some positive affirmations related to the success you will experience. For example, if organization is one of the goals you have laid out following the SMART-ER system, write an affirmation that relates to the success you will have. However, don't write it in the future tense. If you say," I will organize my desk" you will have some difficulty, because the statement is written for the future. It would be more effective to say," My desk is organized, and I am able to locate everything I need and do my work without wasting time hunting for items." You get the idea. Your affirmations should reflect the change you're creating.

Whether you subscribe to the simple, yet profound, wisdom of the ages or whether you follow more contemporary thinking, the message is essentially the same. Each of us is capable of far more than we achieve. Each of us is capable of setting goals that are important to us and each of us is worthy of the success that is ours when we meet those goals. The SMARTER system is a goal setting process that will work wonders for you if you have the ability to hold yourself accountable. A "goal partner" is a great idea as well. You and your goal partner don't even need to be working on the same goals, as long as you check in with each other every week to affirm the progress, determine the next week's goals and encourage each other.

CONNECTING TO THE SPIRITUAL

Prayer Suggestions

- Pray in gratitude for the ability to recognize that you can make some positive changes using the SMART-ER system.

- Pray with thanksgiving that you are paying attention to your conversations. (Remember; it was a chance remark made by my daughter that changed my outlook completely.)

- Pray for those around you that you are influencing by your positive behaviors toward yourself.

- Pray for the self-discipline that you will need to overcome any resistance you may have for the changes you are making.

- Pray for the understanding of an accountability partner who will encourage and support you.

- Pray that you will be the encouragement and support that your accountability partner needs.

PERSONAL MEDITATION

Spend time every day in personal meditation related to the goals you have established. Your subconscious does not have the ability to recognize and process negative statements. Use that knowledge and faith in yourself to repeat affirmations you have written about the success of your goal setting process and progress. For example, if you have established a goal related to better fitness, your affirmations could include statements like these:

- Every day, in every way, I am becoming more fit, with healthier habits of exercise and eating.

- I engage in exercise every day.

- I have more energy for my daily tasks when I am practicing good eating habits.

- I can eat right and exercise right FOR TODAY.

The key to writing and stating positive affirmations is to keep them simple and believable. Be sure to write them in positive terms. Check to be sure they are SMARTER, just like your goals.

SERVING OTHERS
How to Be Available

Serving others and being available to them requires you to focus on more than your own personal goals. However, the successful accomplishment of your goals should benefit those around you as well. For example, if financial health is a goal you are working on, anyone who shares your financial life will benefit. If part of your financial goal includes giving, the benefit will increase in ways you can't imagine at this time. Visualize yourself enjoying the results of your progress. Do you see others in the picture as well? Consider these examples:

- If one of your goals relates to a situation at work or in business that requires more responsibility, won't that benefit your coworkers?

- If one of your goals relates to health and fitness, won't your friends and family benefit, especially if one of them is a walking partner or an exercise buddy?

- If one of your goals relates to monetary gain or financial prosperity, won't your family also benefit from increased financial security?

- If one of your goals relates to a personal desire for growth, won't everyone benefit who will enjoy your efforts, whether they are musical, artistic, or literary?

- If one of your goals relates to your relationships within your family or within your circle of friends, won't that benefit all the people involved as well as anyone either of you associate with?

- If one of your goals relates to contributing your time and/or talent, won't that benefit the recipient of your contribution? An example here might be as simple as volunteering to help with a food drive, a blanket drive, etc.

- If one of your goals relates to recreation, won't that benefit anyone on a team you might coach, anyone who teaches you a new recreational skill, or anyone with whom you share a recreational experience such as a hike?

There are so many ways to apply your goals for the good of others in addition to your own benefit. The ones I've suggested here are meant to trigger your own thinking. People around you may influence you, of course, through your work, your family relationships, your friendships, your community activities or through casual contact. Ultimately, however, the only person who truly can determine your goals is yourself.

PUTTING IT ALL TOGETHER

You can put what you have learned about yourself and what you want to accomplish into practice TODAY. That is the key: do something toward your goals every day. Eleanor Roosevelt said to do something every day that scares you a little bit. She was right. Change and growth can be scary. The point is not to petrify yourself. Petrified things don't move very much! A little sensation of adrenaline gives you "a performer's edge" and helps you focus. Let's get started.

Step One: Go back to the Exercise in this chapter at the end of Section II. Find all your lists.

Step Two: Complete the following Exercise. Notice that the completion of this exercise represents one cycle through the categories of your goals. Upon completion of the first cycle, make whatever adjustments are necessary and work through the cycle again with the same goals or different ones. Remember, as you make your adjustments, the happiest, most satisfied people are those who feel their lives are in balance (or at least in a balanced state that works for them). There is a cliché that states most people do not wish they had spent more time at the office when they look back over their lives.

When you are ready, look back over your lists, and write another list that zeroes in on the most important three or four items in each category. When that is finished, create a chart that has thirteen boxes. Each box will represent one week. In each box, write down two or three of the goals that you have already listed. For example, if a walking program or a fitness program at a gym is on your list, write a starting date down in one of the boxes. You can even code the goals so you are sure that all areas are in focus over the course of each period of three or four weeks. At the end of thirteen weeks, one fourth of a year has gone by. Affirm the progress you have made and repeat the process for the next thirteen weeks.

This is a variation of a method that was used by Benjamin Franklin. He wrote down thirteen character traits or attributes that were important to him. He focused on one attribute each week. By doing so, he could work through his list four times each year. Also, focusing on each one for only one week at a time, he didn't cause himself to burn out or become bored. I think you will find that by applying the thirteen-week system to your desires and goals, you will accomplish much, contribute much, and grow in every area of your life. You can do it, you are worth the effort it takes, and you can be proud of yourself as soon as you take the first step.

Chapter Nine

Improve Your Moral Character

PERSONAL REFLECTION

I am not a sports fan by any stretch of the imagination, but last year I overheard a TV news story that really caught my attention. The story was about the Portland basketball team, The Blazers.

In the story, Paul Allen, owner of the team, was reflecting about the difficulties the team and the organization had during the year. If you live in the Pacific Northwest, you could hardly avoid having heard the many stories about the Blazers' dismal last season – drugs, fights, fines, suspensions, etc. – which culminated in their loss in the very first round of the playoffs.

The Oregonian newspaper posed two key questions in one of its articles: (1) how could a team so fortified with talent be so starved for success? (2) How could a team so loved by its community now be so despised?

Paul Allen, speaking from the wisdom of experience gained the hard way, seemed to have found the answer. He pointed out that his focus during the troubled season had been primarily on the *talent* of the individuals selected for the organization. What he learned in hindsight is that **talent is not enough**! He then made the declaration that in the future he would be looking for both talent and character in the players and in those leading his organization.

I find the story significant because it is indicative of a pivotal challenge for the spiritual person in a commercial world – achieving high levels of professional and financial success without compromising one's spiritual integrity.

Is it possible to be as successful as you'd like, earning as much money as you'd like and still live in integrity with your highest spiritual values?

I like to think that it *is* possible. I believe that spiritual congruence is, indeed, the **only** thing that will make a difference in a society experiencing a crisis of character. I consider a crisis of character exists when materialism – which I define as greed and obsession for money, power, drugs and sex – becomes the compass that guides one's life.

Understand that I am not saying, "Money is evil," or that it is somehow preferable and nobler to live a life of financial destitution and struggle. Rather, I am saying that having our lives founded upon, shaped by and <u>intentionally</u> <u>lived</u> from our deepest values provides the spiritual compass that puts wealth and power into their proper perspectives.

Living with intention requires that we consciously recognize that our lives and our actions have purpose. It requires that we stop pretending that if we "fall asleep" to the best that is within us or allow ourselves to be lulled to sleep by the seduction of the material and the temporal that it won't make any difference.

The cornerstone of living with intention is spiritual congruence: the harmonious alignment and connection of your core values with your thoughts, words and deeds.

Being spiritually congruent is about taking a stand to live fully from your values and highest principles. It is demonstrated by honoring life with the dignity and reverence that lies within you. Spiritual congruence means that you:

- Make decisions that reflect your values and those things that are most important to you
- Exercise choices that flow from your values and honor life
- Take actions that are an outward manifestation of your values

LOOKING INWARD

As we grow older, I don't think many of us actually give much thought to actively building our character or clearly articulating our values. I believe that we take that aspect of our development for granted. I'm not saying that we don't try to live as people with strong moral character or according to a set of principles and values, but I suggest that embarking on an <u>active</u> program of developing our character and aligning our actions with our values will help us create a stronger relationship with ourselves, with others and with Spirit.

One of the most powerful and effective disciplines in which I engage is the practice of taking a daily moral inventory, which I learned from AA. I find that if we keep our goal of becoming the best person we can become consciously in front of us, we minimize the moments that we are tempted to falter. The next page has a template of a daily inventory that you may wish to incorporate into your program of spiritual development.

The other discipline I practice on a yearly basis is that of solidifying my core five values. I define what each value means to me, determine how effectively I am living that value in my life and make the necessary course corrections if my behavior is out of line with my values. Understanding your core values can help you prioritize your life. When you know what is most important to you and what you stand for, it is easier to make decisions about which activities to pursue and which to forego. Knowing your values is an excellent way to bring order and meaning into your life. As you begin to re-orient your life around your values, you will find yourself proactively making room for and enjoying the things that matter most to you.

DAILY INVENTORY

When you retire at night, constructively review your day. Where were you resentful, dishonest, selfish or afraid?

PERSONALITY CHARACTERISTICS OF SELF-WILL Was I ...			PERSONALITY CHARACTERISTICS OF GOD'S-WILL Was I ...
Selfish or Self-Seeking	☐	☐	Interested in Others
Dishonest	☐	☐	Honest
Fearful	☐	☐	Courageous
Inconsiderate	☐	☐	Considerate
Prideful	☐	☐	Humble – Seeking God's Will
Greedy	☐	☐	Giving or Sharing
Angry	☐	☐	Calm/Restrained
Envious	☐	☐	Grateful
Slothful	☐	☐	Action-Oriented
Gluttonous	☐	☐	Exercising Moderation
Impatient	☐	☐	Patient
Intolerant	☐	☐	Tolerant
Resentful	☐	☐	Forgiving
Hateful	☐	☐	Loving – Concerned For Others
Selfish	☐	☐	Generous
Doing Harmful Acts	☐	☐	Doing Good Deeds
Self-Pitying	☐	☐	Self-Forgetful
Self-Justifying	☐	☐	Surrendered
Self-Important	☐	☐	Modest
Self-Condemning	☐	☐	Self-Forgiving
Suspicious	☐	☐	Trusting
Doubtful	☐	☐	Faith-Filled
Deceitful	☐	☐	Truthful

WISDOM FROM THE AGES

The Emperor and the Bride

An emperor in the Far East saw his son growing older and felt that the time had come to choose a bride for his son, as was their culture and custom. Instead of choosing one of the many noble women of good birth in his kingdom, he decided upon a different way of choosing a suitable bride who would be of good character and integrity in order to rule with his son. As part of his plan, he sent out a decree to all the young women of suitable age in the kingdom. His servants were instructed to say, "I have decided it is time to choose a bride for my son. To help me in this process one of my servants will give each one of you a seed today. One very special seed. I want you to plant the seed, water it and come to the palace one year from today with what you have grown from this one seed. I will then judge the plants that you bring, and the owner of the one I choose, will be the bride of my son!"

The people of the kingdom were astounded by this! What WAS the emperor thinking, was he not concerned about noble blood and heritage and their kingdom's customs and traditions? Surely there must be some reason for this...

One young girl named Ling lived in a poor part of town not far from the palace and she, like many others, received a seed. She went home and excitedly told her mother the story. Her mother helped her get a pot and soil, and she planted the seed and watered it carefully. Every day she would water it and watch to see if it had grown. After about three weeks, some of the other young women began to talk about their seeds and the plants that were beginning to grow.

Ling kept checking her seed, but nothing ever grew. Three weeks, four weeks, five weeks went by. Still nothing. By now, others were talking about their plants but Ling didn't have a plant, and she felt like a failure. She wondered if her soil needed some fertilizer but they did not have money for such things. Six months went by - still nothing in Ling's pot. She just knew she must have killed this seed.

Everyone else had trees and tall plants, but she had absolutely nothing to see. Ling didn't say anything to her friends, however. She just kept waiting for her seed to grow. A year finally went by and the time was swiftly approaching when all the young women of the kingdom were to present their plants to the emperor for his inspection. Ling told her mother that she wasn't going; it seemed such a waste to take an empty pot. But her mother said she must be honest about what happened. Ling felt sick to her stomach, but she knew her mother was right. She took her empty pot to the palace.

When Ling arrived, she was amazed at the variety of plants grown by the other women. They were truly beautiful to look at and so pleasing to the eye with all of the many different types of plants in all shapes and sizes that were represented! They were very enterprising projects that were certain to catch the Emperor's attention and sure to reveal their individual abilities as careful and wise gardeners. Justifiably, many were very proud of their personal achievements.

Ling held her empty pot and kept her eyes on the ground in front of her, aware that many of the other young women were pointing, giggling and laughing at her. A few felt sorry for her and offering consolation said, "At least you tried." When the emperor arrived, he surveyed the room and greeted the young women. Ling tried to hide at the back.

"My, what great plants, trees and flowers you have grown," said the emperor. "Today, one of you will be chosen to be the bride of my son who will in turn be emperor of this kingdom!" All of a sudden, as he was speaking, the emperor spotted Ling at the back of the room with her empty pot. He ordered his guards to bring her to the front. Ling was terrified.

"Now the emperor will see that I'm a failure! Maybe he will have me punished or even killed," Ling thought. When Ling got to the front, the Emperor asked her name. "My name is Ling," she replied. All the women and servants were now laughing and making fun of her. The emperor asked everyone to quiet down. He looked at Ling, and then announced to the crowd, "Behold the bride of my son! Her name is Ling!" Ling couldn't believe it. Ling couldn't even grow her seed. She had absolutely nothing to show for her efforts. How could she be the chosen one?

Then the emperor said, "One year ago today, you were each given a seed. I told you to take the seed, plant it, water it, and bring it back to me today. But I gave you all boiled seeds that would not grow. All of you, except Ling, have brought me trees and plants and flowers because when you found that the seed would not grow, you substituted another seed for the one I gave you. Ling was the only one with the courage and honesty to bring me a pot with my true seed in it, untouched and not substituted with any other life. My son will be best served by one with such integrity and purity in both heart and deed. Therefore, she is the one who will be the wife of my son!"

Being a person of superior moral character is a commitment that takes courage and fortitude. It often feels as if it would be so much easier to avoid being conspicuous by taking our cues from how the mainstream operates. When we actively live from our principles, we may find that others jeer at us behind our backs or that we become alienated from the masses. If we stand firm, however, we experience the rewards of personal satisfaction and a deepened connection with Spirit.

We are often presented with opportunities to slow down and reflect on our actions and what we stand for. It is incumbent upon us to be mindful of those moments to reinforce who we wish to be in the world.

KEY THOUGHTS

When you are spiritually congruent, you recognize your connection with something greater than yourself. You pay attention to and nurture that place of connection. You choose to honor the connection by contributing your talent, your power, your time and your wealth in ways that enhance you and the greater field in which you operate: your community, your organization, your family and friends, and God.

By honoring your connection to God, self and others, you make a conscious decision to contribute to the elevation of the human condition – not to its degradation. Those who operate in the world with spiritual congruence build their character in small, unseen ways as well as under the bright light of human scrutiny and judgment.

Spiritual congruence is possible, but it is not always simple. However, there are three key steps you can take to strengthen your ability to live a spiritually connected life.

1. **Clarify:** Clarify your core values. Allow yourself the time to do this. Your values will become a living testament of your character because they determine how you will live. Ask yourself: What brings meaning into my life? What do I really believe in? What do I stand for? What governs my life?

2. **Choose:** Choose to take the courageous actions to stand for your values. Do this despite the fact that you know your choices will be uncomfortable or unpopular. This step requires a leap of faith wherein you trust that by exercising your values-driven convictions, you contribute to your personal greatness and to the greatness of humanity.

3. **Commit:** Commit to living an awakened life. Meditation is just one of the practices in which you can engage that will support you to become more mindful and aware in your moment-to-moment living. Pay attention to those instances where you may be tempted to compromise your values because the call of the material things in your life seems so much louder and more insistent.

CONNECTING TO THE SPIRITUAL

Assessing your moral character as a regular daily practice is a discipline that needs to be conducted with objectivity, compassion towards yourself and forgiveness for the areas in which you fall short.

Taking your moral inventory should be done as dispassionately as possible. An inventory takes stock of what is on hand – not just on what needs to be replenished. In addition to determining areas for continued improvement, it is crucial that you acknowledge the areas in which you consistently make choices that are reflective of your highest spiritual principles.

Noting your progress along with your continued challenges will help you put your spiritual development into the proper perspective. It will also keep your spirit energized and moving forward with anticipation.

The primary impetus behind the development of our character defects is fear. We fear that we may lose something we already have or fail to get something we want. In all cases, as you work on your moral character development, use prayer to ask for help and guidance to remove your character defects, and to express your gratitude for whom you are becoming.

Prayer Suggestions

In your prayer life:

- Pray for the removal or transformation of your fears

- Pray for clear sight so you can keep your mind focused on what is most important

- Pray for courage and fearlessness

- Pray for the strength to stand by your values and principles

- Pray for the wisdom to handle the "gray areas" of your life with integrity

Transforming your character defects will require concerted effort on your part. Some of your defects in character will be more obstinate than others. It is essential that as you stay focused on your ideal, you understand that the goal is **progress**, not **perfection**.

PERSONAL MEDITATION

The Prayer of St. Francis

Lord, make me a channel of thy peace – that where there is hatred, I may bring love – that where there is wrong, I may bring the spirit of forgiveness – that where there is discord, I may bring harmony – that where there is error, I may bring truth – that where there is doubt, I may bring faith – that where there is despair, I may bring hope – that where there are shadows, I may bring light – that where there is sadness, I may bring joy.

Lord, grant that I may seek to comfort, rather than to be comforted – to understand, rather than to be understood – to love, than to be loved.

For it is by self-forgetting that one finds. It is by forgiving that one is forgiven. It is by dying that one awakens to Eternal Life. Amen.

The practice of strengthening our moral character at times demands that we allow our old image of ourselves to die. We must be willing to sacrifice our comfort in knowing who we are for the initial discomfort of growing toward who we can become. Willingness is a key factor in our endeavor to improve our moral character. The Prayer of St. Francis is an inspired prayer you can use as a meditation. Record yourself reading this prayer and play the recording at the beginning of your meditation period. Allow the words to engulf you as you envision yourself becoming the channel of peace referenced in the prayer.

SERVING OTHERS
How to Be Available

Being a person of strong moral character and integrity means that we recognize that we belong to a greater whole than our separate existences would seem to imply. Our focus moves away from us – from our self-centered, private wants and desires – to how we can touch others and touch God.

Humility, our willingness to be led by Spirit, is a key ingredient in working with our character shortcomings. Humility is the foundation for creating a serene relationship with life. Indeed, humility is what transforms us from self-centered creatures seeking only comfort and material advantage, to people who put their spiritual values at the center of all their accomplishments.

As we grow in humility, we become more approachable and open to others and we learn how to create more harmonious lives. Being of strong character allows us to spread harmonious influences and teaches those around us that it is possible to prosper as a spiritual person in a material world.

PUTTING IT ALL TOGETHER

Character development allows us to keep our spiritual values consciously and intentionally in front of us. Create a daily practice wherein you:

1. Identify your character flaws and work to correct them

2. Acknowledge and allow yourself to feel remorse for harming yourself or others

3. Express gratitude for the blessings you receive in your life

4. Cultivate the willingness to continue to make progress toward your ideal

Chapter Ten

Achieve Your Potential

PERSONAL REFLECTION

As an adult, I look back on my childhood on a self-sustaining farm with humble gratitude for the lessons I absorbed from my family and yes, from the farm animals, the gardens, and the orchards. My parents had a sense of stewardship and respect for the natural world and its abundance that awes me now. Of course, as a youngster, I took all of it for granted, assuming that all little boys and girls had the same experiences I did. When I realized that even my friends who lived in town didn't know what I was talking about when I mentioned hoeing, weeding, slopping the pigs, and mucking out the barns, I would have gladly traded their life for mine. I remember telling my parents that "I would never make my kids live on a farm and do all this work!" They just smiled and reminded me that the strawberries...all five acres...were mine to hoe.

Now I live on ten acres of that original farm. We raised our children here and even though it was no longer a self-sustaining farm and their chores were very different from mine, it was still a "country style" childhood that they experienced. Living close to the land offers a unique perspective on what is important, what can wait, and what can't. The victories, the failures, and the opportunities for second chances were a critical part of farm life.

LOOKING INWARD

It has been said "for everything there is a season". We often consider that statement to be an allegory to the various seasons of our lives, from youth and its spring-like promise to the harvest and dormancy of our later years. However, for our purpose here, I'd like us to think about the seasons as parts of the goal setting process.

Imagine that the **season of spring** is like the birth of a new idea, a new opportunity to set a goal. We understand that setting a goal requires some promises to yourself. There must be a specific statement of the desired outcome. The results must be measurable. The accomplishment must be achievable and realistic. There must be an expected date of accomplishment with perhaps some benchmark dates and benchmark accomplishments along the way. There must be a statement of what you are willing "to pay" for the achievement, in terms of time, sacrifice, etc.

The **summer season** is the time of activities that will lead to the satisfaction of the goal you have set. This is the time to make note of the lesser objectives that make up the goal. This is also the time for the adjustments that you might need to make for the eventual fruition.

Fall is the season during which the harvest is reaped. The harvest you reap from the original goal may be somewhat different than you originally expected. You may receive more than you expected or less than you expected, but nevertheless there will be a harvest.

The **winter season** provides a time to reflect on your accomplishments, a time for a period of dormancy, and a time to assess the previous harvest. It is a time to replenish yourself.

The most important idea here is that spring follows winter! Again you have an opportunity to set a goal and to move it through the seasons. I am not saying that you can only work on one goal at a time. You may have many goals reflecting various areas of your life. You may be working in different seasons with each of the goals.

124

This is good because if you have several goals and they're all in "summer" you may exhaust yourself to the point of frustration and burnout.

The Goal-Setting Cycle

Spring Planting the seed	Establishing a new goal, birthing a new idea or beginning a new endeavor.
Summer Farming the seed	Getting into action, making needed adjustments and implementing new strategies
Fall Harvesting the crop	Reaping the benefits of your activities and celebrating your accomplishments
Winter Preparing for dormancy	Reflecting upon and assessing the outcomes of your actions and rejuvenating yourself

Let me share a personal example of this process. My husband encouraged me to take clarinet lessons with him. I was and still am a singer and can pick out some things on the piano. I had never played any other instrument. This was a new idea! (spring). We had an opportunity to join a band that was just forming, made up primarily of people over the age of fifty. The band director was a retired music educator who was still very active in local theater productions as a music leader and who still played "gigs" around town quite frequently. We were in good hands.

I set a goal to be playing first clarinet in five years or less. My benchmarks would be moving from third clarinet, to second and ultimately to first clarinet as new music was passed out. I was willing to "pay" in terms of dedication to practice, asking for help when I needed it, and maintaining a positive attitude through the "screeching stage". Spring flowed into summer as I continued to learn new notes, new techniques, and gained confidence. My fall harvest has been recently fulfilled as I find the director almost always gives me first clarinet music whenever new music is passed out. This is a major victory. It has been less than four years and I have earned the respect of my fellow musicians, my director, and myself. Now what? Rather than "going dormant" through the winter of this goal, or perhaps abandoning it as "done", my choice is to refine the original goal. My new goal in this area is to earn the right to have a solo part in some of our music. As I often tell myself in situations like this…"Why not?" and "Who's going to stop me?"

By the way, as I mentioned earlier, I believe you need to have a series of goals relating to various aspects of your life in different seasons of fruition. Therefore, I have set goals for fitness and weight management, goals to enhance my relationship with my husband, goals related to nurturing my friendships, goals for what I want to do to our house, goals for our flowers and landscaping, goals for maintaining close family ties with our adult children and grandchildren, and so on. You may be thinking "goals…shmoals" , but let me elaborate just a bit more. I believe that a vague idea of something you want to improve or change is not a goal. I believe that in order for a dream or an idea to be a real goal it must meet certain criteria. Goals need to be SMARTER…specific, measurable, achievable, reasonable, time bound, energizing, and rewarded. The only way to accomplish this is to write them down. That's right… write them down.

However we approach the concept of goal setting and however we keep track of our progress is a personal choice. Do what works for you. The key concept here is that we are building our own future, day by day and one decision at a time. Here is a story that will emphasize this point.

WISDOM FROM THE AGES

The Builder

An elderly carpenter was ready to retire. He told his employer-contractor of his plans to leave the house building business and live a more leisurely life with his wife enjoying his extended family. He would miss the paycheck, but he needed to retire. They could get by.

The contractor was sorry to see his good worker go and asked if he could build just one more house as a personal favor. The carpenter said yes, but in time it was easy to see that his heart was not in his work. He resorted to shoddy workmanship and used inferior materials. It was an unfortunate way to end his career.

When the carpenter finished his work and the contractor came to inspect the house, he handed the front-door key to the carpenter. "This is your house," he said, "my gift to you."

What a shock! What a shame! If he had only known he was building his own house, he would have done it all so differently. Now he had to live in the home he had built none too well.

KEY THOUGHTS

Do these examples resonate with you? Sometimes we build our lives in a distracted way, reacting rather than acting, willing to put up less than the best. At important points we do not give the job our best effort. Then with a shock we look at the situation we have created and find that we are now living in the house we have built. If we had realized, we would have done it differently.

Think of yourself as the carpenter. Think about your house. Each day you hammer a nail. Place a board, or erect a wall. Build wisely. It is the only life you will ever build. Even if you live it for only one more day, that day deserves to be lived at your best, with grace and dignity. The plaque on the wall says," Life is a do-it-yourself project." This is very clear. Your life today is the result of your attitudes and choices in the past. Your life tomorrow will be the result of your attitudes and choices you make today.

CONNECTING TO THE SPIRITUAL

Prayer Suggestions

- Pray in praise of the desire you feel for improving an aspect of your life.

- Pray with thanksgiving for the ability you have for acting on a desire you have.

- Pray with gratitude for the positive steps you have taken.

- Pray with hope for the vision you are creating for yourself.

- Pray for those around you whom you are influencing through the positive changes you are experiencing and will experience.

- Pray for the strength you will need to deal with the temptations you will face as you work for change.

- Pray for a generous heart, that you may be a force for good in your relationships to friends, family, community, and the world.

- Pray for an attitude of gratitude as you assess your work so far.

PERSONAL MEDITATION

Spend time every day in personal meditation related to the goals you are working on and the season each goal reflects. Affirm the progress you have made and visualize the goal moving ever forward toward the next season. If you are experiencing a plateau, notice it but do not draw undo attention to it. Your subconscious does not acknowledge the negative word attached to an admonition. For example, if you have backslid (and we all have), don't say to yourself, "Don't do that again." Your subconscious will zero in on "Do that again" and you know what happens next!

You might want to write out some positive affirmations or statements related to the progress you have been noticing and what you want to do next. An example might be:

- Every day in every way I am getting stronger about keeping my commitment to myself.
- I can see that I am making progress toward my goal and I am proud of myself for the work I'm doing.
- I am making time (not finding it) to notice what I'm thinking about and what I'm doing about my goal. (It's probably wise to state what the goal is each time, instead of just calling it a goal. Your subconscious likes you to be very specific, especially since you have more than one goal by now.)

You get the idea. The affirmations don't have to be long or elaborate. They do, however, need to be written in positive rather than negative terms. They should be SMARTER, just like the goal itself.

SERVING OTHERS
How to Be Available

How can you serve others while working on goals of your own? How will the accomplishment of your goal benefit those around you? Consider these examples.

- If one of your goals relates to improving your relationship with a friend or family member, won't that benefit both of you as well as anyone else either of you associate with?
- If one of your goals relates to learning a new skill such as playing an instrument, couldn't that benefit the people who will enjoy your musical offerings?
- If one of your goals has to do with home improvement and/or landscaping, won't that benefit your entire neighborhood?
- If one of your goals has to do with volunteering in your community, won't that benefit everyone who receives your volunteer services?
- If one of your goals has to do with spiritual practice, won't that benefit your community of believers?
- If one of your goals has to do with health and fitness, won't your family benefit?

You get the idea. Visualize yourself enjoying the benefits of your goal yourself and you will be able to visualize others in the picture as well.

PUTTING IT ALL TOGETHER

Are you ready to get started? Think about all the areas of your life and the roles you play in those areas. List them, leaving space between. For example, one area might be family member. Your roles might include spouse (husband or wife), parent (mom or dad), grandparent, aunt or uncle, brother or sister, niece or nephew, son or daughter, grandson or granddaughter.

Another area might be "worker". Your roles might include boss or employee, supervisor, steward, associate, commuter.

Still another area might be "volunteer". Your roles could include driver, club officer or member, scout leader or assistant, school volunteer, or any number of other activities you perform that benefit your neighborhood or community.

Can you see why you are exhausted? You probably do way more than you thought. Decide where you want to begin making some positive changes. You may even realize that some of the roles you play are not satisfying a need for you or others. It's OK to prioritize and drop some activities to focus on others.

Think about the seasons as they apply to what you are doing. Can you find evidence of spring, summer, fall and winter? If so, you are living the seasons. If not, this is an opportunity to create SMARTER goals. Whatever you discover about yourself and the process, focus on affirming what you are doing well. Ask for feedback and suggestions. Most of all, remember that the natural seasons flow into and out of each other. Even on the stormiest days the sun can peek through.

PART IV

RECOGNIZING AND REAFFIRMING YOUR BLESSINGS

Chapter Eleven

Give Back to Yourself First

PERSONAL REFLECTION

When I was a young woman, it occurred to me that my parents had done an amazing job of modeling their roles as parents, spouses, friends, citizens of their community and spirit-filled children of God. Example after example of how I wanted to be "when I grew up" was laid out before me. The powerful part for me as I look back as an adult was that it wasn't particularly intentional. That's just the way it was. Most families in our community functioned pretty much as ours did. This was during the fifties and it was certainly a different time. My parents were married during the depression and I was born just before the end of World War II. As I matured into a young woman with a family of my own, I remember asking my mom and dad how I could ever repay them for the lessons learned. I'll never forget my mom's response. She said, "You can never pay back all the blessings of your life. All you can do is pass them on." A popular movie portrayed this concept as well. Perhaps you saw it. It was called "Pay it Forward".

LOOKING INWARD

Let's draw an analogy between passing on our blessings and the concept of emergency oxygen masks on aircraft. No matter which airline you're flying or where you are in the world, the directions are the same. Put on your oxygen mask first and then assist those around you. The core concept to understanding this is that it is not selfish to take care of yourself first. What is the lesson here?

I think the most powerful message is that you must continuously replenish yourself. You can only give from your own abundance. That abundance of emotional well-being, spiritual well-being, and physical well-being creates a flow that you can actually feel. When you take care of yourself before you give to everyone around you, it's like living on the interest instead of the principle. Do you remember when people were able to live on the interest from their investments? When the economy was healthier, people weren't concerned about depleting their principle. Living on the interest is sustainable. So is giving from your abundance. Let me clarify further. This giving is not about money and the reference to the economy was only to make a point.

The question remains. How do you replenish yourself? The answer is individual, personal, and variable. The answer also depends upon what it is that you are giving. For example, if you are giving time, you must find a way to replenish yourself in terms of time. Imagine this scenario and try to apply it to your circumstances: You have a huge project---one that will consume you for days. How do you approach it? Do you slavishly hunker down, grit your teeth, and attack the project until you're exhausted, angry or frustrated? Or, do you work as hard as you can and stay totally focused for 45 to 60 minutes and then take a real break for 15 to 20 minutes before resuming your efforts? Where will you be at the end of a day? I would bet that the work hard/take a break routine will get you farther even though it may seem ludicrous to "break" that much.

Here's the magic. When you are "taking a break" at the conscious level with a walk, a nap, a novel, or anything of choice, your subconscious is still at work, assessing what you've done, determining adjustments, and planning strategies. How does it do that? You tell it to, at the conscious level. Does it work? Yes it does. Does it take practice? Yes it does. Is it worthwhile? Yes it is. The times I've suggested here are only examples. The concept remains, however. Real effort should flow into a real break and back into real effort that is renewed and energized.

The other concept remains as well. Guard your principle. Share from your abundance (the interest on your principle).

WISDOM FROM THE AGES

Throughout history, in the wisdom literature of many religions and philosophies, in poetry, in letters to individuals and to groups, and in many other examples, we can find the same concept that my mother shared with me. The concept of passing the best on is an agricultural gem as well as a way of living. A powerful example is to be found in the Gospel of Luke 6:38. "Give to others and God will give to you. Indeed, you will receive a full measure, a generous helping, poured into your hands---all that you can hold. The measure that you use for others is the one that God will use for you." Can you see the power in these statements? The power that is reserved for you? It's there in the last part—"the measure that you use for others is the one that God will use for you." When we give our best, we need to be ready to receive the best.

We must apply the "faith without works" philosophy here. Faith is a wonderful, powerful force, but we are required to do our part. Even though we will receive "a full measure, a generous helping" we must work to replenish ourselves as well. How do you do that? Again, this is a very personal choice. You can give yourself time, solitude, peace, energy, focus, goals, learning, and many other gifts. In fact, you can give yourself the most important gift of all. Whatever it is that will replenish you.

KEY THOUGHTS

Wait just a minute, you may be saying. "Do you have any idea how busy I am? I'd like to see you try to 'replenish' yourself on my schedule." You can start from where you are and you can start any time you decide that you are worth the choice of replenishment. How? I'm going to share two scenarios—one for people who work outside their homes and one for people who work from home. Before you get frustrated with me, let me say that I know **everybody** works at home! I'm talking here about people who come home from work to the zillion tasks that remain to be done every day. I'm also talking about people who really do work from home and still "come home" to the zillion tasks that remain to be done every day.

First, for the people who work outside their homes, please respond to the following questions.

- How do you get to work? How long does it take? How do you use the time it takes to get to work? Is there an opportunity there to replenish yourself? Could you listen to a book on tape or a CD that would serve to replenish you in ways that would be meaningful? There are hundreds of books and other inspiring materials available for your university on wheels. Perhaps music is a key to the way you replenish yourself. Tapes, CDs, and the radio might be available to you. I would not recommend a talk show format, unless someone else's "beef" is inspiring to you. My bias is showing here, I know, but the point of this is to replenish your store of inspiration, learning, and energy, not to further diminish it.

- How do you use your break time at work? Do you work through your break? Do you grab a bite on the run, so to speak, and continue with your work routine? I think you will find that if you take a real break, whenever you are entitled to one, you will return to your work with renewed energy and optimism for the tasks to be done. If you eat lunch and take other breaks in the company of pleasant people who are interesting to talk with, your energy will be restored as well. I have worked in the company of pleasant and unpleasant people myself. I would go away from some conversations so depressed and/or frustrated and/or angry that I would lose valuable time away from my tasks, reflecting on the negative energy I had just experienced. On the other hand, I would go away from some conversations renewed, re-energized, and ready to take on the world, or at least my next task. I realized that the conversations I engaged in were my choice. Of course, you may still have to work with unpleasant people, as I did, but you shouldn't have to take your breaks with them unless you want to. Is there another place and/or another time to take a break? Take a book, write a letter, pay your bills, or do some other "obvious" task.

- How do you use your "wait time"? Everybody I know has at least some time when they are waiting for an appointment for themselves or someone else, waiting for someone like a child who is in some kind of practice situation, waiting to board a plane, and so on and so on. Do you engage in something productive or do you pick up a years-old magazine and idly page through it? There's nothing wrong with that, of course, if it frees your mind and helps you relax. However, many people find that frustrating and long for a simple solution. Have you tried filling a small tote with things to do? You could include letters you need to answer that are not urgent, envelopes to address, advertising flyers you use to make out your grocery lists, etc. Your only limitation here is what you can easily manage to tote around. One of my daughters takes small mending tasks, such as replacing buttons, etc. Not every place is convenient for that kind of task, so you'll have to be the judge. My opinion is anything you can do "out" is one less thing you have to do at home. Why not give it a try?

- When you are at home, do you multitask, or at least let your appliances multitask? Do you make a practice of running your washer, dryer, and dishwasher at the same time? If they all need to be run, why not do them together? Hot water isn't really an issue, because most dishwashers heat the water anyway. You may only gain a few minutes by doing this, but a few minutes almost every day adds up very quickly. There are lots of ways to multitask at home with regard to your chores that will build in small efficiencies. You might even want to share your ideas with a friend and see if the two of you can think of even more. Women's magazines and columns are full of hints like these. I'm always a little amused when I read them; maybe you are, too. Don't you find that you've already been doing some of the hints you read for years?

For the people who work at home, the suggestions here might be helpful to you as well. I think in some ways that you have a more difficult situation when it comes to replenishing yourself. At home, there are so many tasks, both large and small, that beg for our attention every time we take a break from our "real job", or at least the one we're getting paid to perform. It's critical that you give yourself whatever gift of time you can manage, even if you have to put it on your list of things that have to be done.

I am a convinced list maker. When I don't jot down my plans for the day, I get very little accomplished and what's worse, I don't know what I did last week or last month. When I do have my daily list, I am more likely to get everything done I intended to do, with plenty of time to spare. Further, I can look back on previous lists (I keep mine in a little journal) and see all that I have accomplished over the period of a year, a month, or a week. I find that journal in itself to be replenishing and inspiring. My lists are not exciting; they have listings such as laundry, bills, letters, cleaning, practicing my clarinet, where I'm speaking, my daily 15 minutes of writing, etc. My husband and I have "dates" every week, when we'll go for a hike, to a museum, to a movie, and so on. Those are listed as well. It really is fun to see what we've done, when our memories would fail us.

CONNECTING TO THE SPIRITUAL

Consider the abundance of your life. Giving back to yourself first is like the wise farmer who saves his best seeds from each crop and the best animals from each birthing cycle. He then preserves and protects that which is the best and most fruitful so that it can be replanted to create the next abundant harvest. Our gifts and talents are the best we have been given and the best that we can give to others. They are our "best seeds."

- Think about harvesting, preserving, and replanting the best seed. What are your best seeds? How do you harvest, preserve, and replant that which is in you?
  Keys to getting started with this idea:
  1. Write down 10 of your best qualities and/or values
  2. Reflect on the previous question with regard to these qualities/values.
  3. How are they manifested in your life, in your relationships, etc?

- How do you take care of yourself so you can continue to share from your abundance?
- Think about the analogy to the oxygen masks on the airplane. Who needs you to put on your mask before you can help them? How do you make it clear that you have to get your "oxygen" first?

Prayer Suggestions

- Pray in thanksgiving for the abundance in your life.

- Pray for the people whose lives have touched yours.

- Pray for those who have guided your path.

- Pray for the harvest of your best seeds.

- Pray for the preserving of your best seeds, whatever they may be.

- Pray for the replanting of your best seeds in the life of someone else.

- Pray for the replenishment of your capital, as you give back to yourself.

PERSONAL MEDITATION

As you pray, you are engaging in powerful personal meditation. As you open your mind to spirit-filled energy, your thoughts will flow. While you are relaxed and receptive, your subconscious mind will reveal random thoughts that you are only marginally aware of. Pay attention to these quiet times. Profound ideas will occur to you, seemingly "out of the blue." You may want to jot down some of these ideas, even though at the time they may not appear to be relevant to your situation. If negative self-talk appears when your guard is down, notice it and counter it with positive affirmations about yourself and the progress you are making. Continue to visualize yourself as relaxed, confident, energized, and fulfilled. Use your quiet time to appreciate the gifts you have been given: the ability to nurture yourself and others, the ability to make use of your talents in the service of others as well as yourself, the ability to learn from your experiences, even if they were mistakes. There are many ways to use a period of meditation. At first, until you develop the habit, you may find your mind focusing on the other things you "should" be doing. It takes practice and self-discipline to keep your mind relaxed, receptive, and positive. It is worth the work it takes. You are worth the work it takes.

SERVING OTHERS
How to Be Available

How can you serve others while you are giving back to yourself first? It seems like a paradox to state that by replenishing yourself first you are serving others in a way that will not reduce your capital. I mentioned before that it is important to guard your capital. In other words, give from "the interest" in terms of your energy, your time, and your talents. As you work to replenish yourself in any way that works for you, you are actually increasing your capital of energy, time, and talent and will ultimately have more to give.

Try this exercise:

1. List one important way that you have given of yourself yesterday or today. Remember, your time is as much a gift as any other talent. Note the time, energy, empathy, etc. that you gave and to whom.

2. List the way in which you will give what you gave away back to yourself, gift for gift.

3. Continue this process until you have exhausted all the ways in which you have given of yourself for the time period you chose.

4. Tally the time, the energy, and the empathy in separate columns. (Some things take a lot of time but not much energy. Of course the reverse is also true.)

5. Compare that approach to trying to do too much without taking care of yourself. It is sad but true that terminal patients often outlive their caregivers unless the caregivers have been very proactive about taking care of themselves and replenishing the energy, empathy, and so on that they are expending. On a less dramatic note, we can all learn from this example. Take care of yourself; renew what needs to be renewed so that you don't burn out. Give back to yourself first and you will always have the best seeds available to share with others.

PUTTING IT ALL TOGETHER

The law of reciprocity is as real as the law of gravity. When you give to others, you will be the recipient of abundant gifts in return. You reap what you sow. Sow time, and you will receive time; sow empathy and you will receive empathy; sow kindness, caring and nurturing and you will receive the same or better. When you give back to yourself, you are insuring that you will never run out of what it is that you are giving. Put this concept into practice this week. When you have taken the time to prepare for the outcome that you desire and you've done your best, there is hope. Hope is desire accompanied by expectation.

There are so many exercises listed in this material. You may have thought of more that you can do on an ongoing basis. That is key; keep up with the exercises that work for you. When you need a change in your outlook, go back to some of the exercises that didn't seem relevant before. Perhaps, as you've grown, these exercises will prove more relevant than they did. Whatever paths you follow to giving back to yourself first, have a pleasant journey.

Chapter Twelve

Harness Your Power

PERSONAL REFLECTION

"The task before us is no match for the power behind us." I first read that quote on a church reader board, and it really resonated with me. I got to thinking that a simple sentence like that can be life-changing in the impact it has on us and in the way we choose to apply it. The more I thought about the impact of that statement, the more I wondered how I could employ it to guide my relationships, my personal goals, and my capacity to nurture a spirit-filled life.

As I pondered the significance of that train of thought, my musings took me back to my childhood yet again. I can remember having enormous stage fright before a piano recital even when I was "too young to have stage fright." Most of the other little kids in my piano teacher's studio could hardly wait to show their parents and the rest of us what they could do, even if it was a one-fingered melody. On the other hand, I was terrified. My terror was nameless, faceless, and to this day I can't describe it. I don't think I was afraid of making a mistake. I don't think I was afraid of what the other little kids would think. I honestly have no idea what scared me so.

My dad told me something that saved me then and saves me today when I am tempted to give in to my fears. He said, "None of the people in this room can play your piece just like you can." What a simple statement! How true it is to consider that no one can "play our piece" just like we can. That takes me right back to the opening statement. Playing our piece is simply another name for the task before us.

LOOKING INWARD

I believe there are three distinct origins of the *power behind us.*

1. The first of these great origins is the power of **tradition.** In any area of our lives, there are traditions that shape our response to the circumstances and even, in some cases, keep us from responding. Tradition can be a powerful force, but it doesn't need to stop us. In fact, traditions can be a launching pad for changes that will benefit us and everyone around us. Many of us have experienced the effort it takes to start new family traditions. A newly married couple may want to have their own holiday practices, for example.

   In business, and in other areas, we can use tradition as a launching pad as well, but still put our own unique stamp on our work. Think of other areas in which tradition plays an important role in your decision-making. Does it limit you or launch you? You get to decide!

2. The second of these great origins is the power of **experience.** We need not rely solely on our own experience. The experiences of others allow us to rely on people who have *"been there, done that"*. This can be sort of a velvet trap. On the one hand, it can be reassuring to know that someone else has done what you need to do and you can lean on that experience. However, sometimes experience can sound like *"we've never done it that way"*. It isn't always easy to get the advice and help we seek, but still maintain our independence and style. Here again, the experience of other people and even your own prior experience can limit you or launch you. Once again, you get to decide!

3. I believe the greatest of all the powers behind you is the **power within you**. Call it spirituality, desire, ambition, the desire for lifelong learning, the commitment to excellence, or any other term that works for you. All of us have a built in (God given) sense of self. If yours has been under a basket for a while, it's time to peek under there, drag it out, and tell yourself, **"The task before me is no match for the power behind me."**

WISDOM FROM THE AGES

One of my favorite folktales when I was a little girl is the one about the contest between the wind and the sun. Each of them believed himself to be the most powerful force in nature and refused to acknowledge the power of the other.

One day the wind and the sun decided to have a contest. The winner of the contest would claim to be the most powerful force of nature and the loser would have to agree with that claim.

They even argued about the kind of contest they would have. Finally they noticed a man walking along a path and decided that the winner would be the one who could force the man to take off his jacket.

The wind tried first. He sent out a gentle breeze to try to blow off the man's jacket. The man merely closed the jacket with its fasteners. The wind blew harder and harder, but the man clung ever more fiercely to his jacket. Finally, the wind conceded defeat, exhausted and frustrated that he had not been able to prevail over the man.

The sun took his turn. He sent out warm rays and beamed upon the man. The man smiled, turned his face up to the sun and relaxed his hold on his jacket. The sun turned up the heat, little by little, the man relaxed more and more, and before long had removed his jacket.

The sun declared himself the winner.

KEY THOUGHTS

You may wonder how this story relates to the idea of the power within you to accomplish a task. At first glance, both the wind and the sun appear to be outside influences. The sun, however, with its warmth, stimulates a response within the man, encouraging him to smile, to turn his face to the sun, and to remove his jacket. I appreciate the imagery of that scene.

It's a similar response to the power within us that encourages us to smile, to turn our thoughts and minds upward, and to remove the reluctance we feel to make a positive change in our lives.

Change is never particularly easy for most of us. It's a symbolic abandonment of what is familiar, even if the familiar is not allowing growth. Focus on the origins of your personal power, the traditions, the experiences, and your inner strength to make the changes that you desire. Give yourself credit for the work that you have done to improve yourself up to now. Education, reading, positive relationships, volunteering, learning new skills, and all the other aspects of the development of a well-rounded person will serve you every time you desire to make additional changes.

CONNECTING TO THE SPIRITUAL

Consider the areas of your life in which **tradition** seems to play an important part. Under each area, think about the traditions that influence you. Some of these traditions may work for you and some may limit you. There are ways to change the ones that limit you by changing what you say to yourself about them. Be careful in your self-talk not to sabotage yourself.

Focus on the areas in which your own prior **experience**, or the experience of someone else, plays an important part. You can find that limiting, or you can take advantage of it as a launching pad. Many of the world's greatest contributors stood on the shoulders of those who had gone before and influenced them. It is within our power to achieve greatness based on someone else's preliminary work and thought.

Finally, think about the **power within you.** What ambitions, dreams, goals, or desires can you bring to bear on your new tasks?

Prayer Suggestions

- Pray in thanksgiving for the traditions that support you.

- Pray for those whose traditions inspired you to achieve more.

- Pray in thanksgiving for the experiences of others that have empowered you.

- Pray in thanksgiving for your own experiences that are leading you forward.

- Pray in thanksgiving for the ambitions you feel.

- Pray for courage and determination to set goals based on your ambitions and dreams.

- Pray in thanksgiving for your new tasks.

PERSONAL MEDITATION

The power that is bestowed on us when we pray with a spirit-filled heart cannot be underestimated. As our minds are opened and receptive, new thoughts flood in. Be aware of these seemingly random and fleeting thoughts. They are the stuff of genius. Everyone's mind is capable of tremendous thought; not everyone pays attention. Everyone is capable of paying attention; not everyone will form good intentions. Everyone is capable of acting on his or her good intentions; not everyone will. That is the key. Pray, receive, attend, intend, act. All five of these action- filled concepts can be developed over time. Some of these attributes may be fully developed in you through the force of habit. All of us can develop more fully in the habits of prayer, in receptivity, in paying attention to our thoughts, in developing good intentions, and in acting on those good intentions. It is work worthy of a spirit-filled life. You are worthy of the fulfillment of the power within you.

SERVING OTHERS
How to Be Available

How can you serve others while you are developing the ability to use the traditions given to you? How can you serve others while you are focusing on the benefits of the experiences of others as well as your own? How can you serve others while you are paying attention to the power within you? It is important to recognize that those around you have traditions of their own, experiences of their own, and a power within themselves as well. You can help by talking about your own journey, modeling what it means to live a spirit-filled life based on tradition, experience, and power, and encouraging those with whom you have positive relationships.

Enter into new relationships with the anticipation that you will add value to the other person's life as they will add value to yours. Great relationships are mutually beneficial. You have as much to offer as the other person. Learn to see yourself as the epitome of all that has preceded you culturally, artistically, socially, and in other ways in your background. When you have doubts about the value you bring to a relationship, take heart in the thought that we all struggle with these ideas. You are worthy. You can best serve others by taking your eyes off yourself. This is not subservience; far from it. False humility is as dangerous to a developing mind as false pride. Be proud of yourself and what you have to offer. No one on this planet can offer what you can, in the same way you can.

PUTTING IT ALL TOGETHER

Use everything you have gained as you work toward your definition of a spirit-filled life. You have the traditions of the ages. Give yourself permission to use every tradition that appeals to you and that works for you. You have the experience of everyone you have heard about or read about. Bring to bear on your tasks what all of those people have learned. Give yourself permission to use all that the heroes of the ages learned through their experiences. Ask yourself, "What would (fill in the blank with the name of anyone you admire from the beginning of time) do in this situation?"

All of that tradition and experience that you are learning to depend on and to use leads directly to the power that you already have within you. I've always thought that somewhere on this earth someone has the answer to lasting world peace. They just haven't recognized it yet. Is it you?

Chapter Thirteen

Affirm Your Greatness

PERSONAL REFLECTION

When I was a little girl, I came to depend so much on excuses that they became a real crutch for me. For example, if my mom or dad caught me doing something I wasn't supposed to do, I would claim that "Honey told me to do that." Honey was my imaginary friend, as real to me as anything else in my life. Most of the time, Honey was my confidante, my comfort, and my emotional support. Sometimes, however, Honey was the brat I secretly wanted to be. As I got older and Honey "moved away", I often wished with all my heart that Honey was back in my life. It would have been so handy, when I got my first speeding ticket, missed curfew at the sorority house, and all the other escapades that lured me into trouble. I never did anything really bad, but I always knew that Honey was the only one who would have understood completely why I had done what I did. Excuses, for most of us, are the explanations we give to ourselves and to others for the things that don't turn out quite right or quite the way we had hoped.

LOOKING INWARD

Excuses! Don't you just love them? Excuses are our friends, protecting us from unwanted activities, unwanted relationships, unwanted anything.

I don't know how you reacted to that statement.....I don't think it went over very well, so let's try this one. *"When you make a list of excuses, be sure your name is on the list".* Not any better, is it?

The truth is, excuses mainly serve to deny us an experience, a relationship, a learning opportunity, or an opportunity to grow. A current sports campaign says, "Feel the fear and do it anyway". I'm not saying that I haven't used an excuse as a friend and protector, because I have. I have found, however, that many of the excuses that were "tried and true" became the reasons for doing the thing. For example, saying "I don't have time to attend a seminar" is the very reason to attend. You will probably learn the strategy you need to have the time you want. *"I don't have the time and energy to exercise"* is another one I frequently hear (I used to use that one myself). I have found that exercising gives me the energy and the reflection time I need to make many decisions that affect the rest of my day.

One way to deal with this very difficult area of our lives is to return to the concept of self-talk, notice it, make note of it, and then work to shift the paradigm in each statement. For the longest time, I didn't realize that my self-talk often took the form of excuses that prevented me from moving forward.

We have also talked about harnessing the power of tradition, experience and the power within. If your personal tradition is one of excuses, you will find that you have some work to do. You might want to work on this with a trusted friend. You may not be aware of the excuses you use, because of the habit and tradition of using them. Your friend may be able to point them out when you use them. This is a pretty big risk and can lead to even more "defensive" excuses or statements of denial. This is natural, so you both need to be aware of the potential for unhappy feelings as you work to learn to recognize the pattern. Keep working, though; it's worth the effort.

WISDOM FROM THE AGES

Throughout recorded history, the literature, folklore, and common tales of most cultures have used the concept of excuses and how they can get people into trouble as morality lessons. Remember Eve's excuse? "The serpent told me to…" Remember Adam's excuse? "Eve told me to…. Remember the stories that ended "and the moral of the story is…" One of the stories that has always resonated with me is the following one. I think the lesson here is as appropriate today for me as an adult as it was years ago when I was a little girl.

Persephone

Demeter had the care of all the plants, fruits, and grains in the world. She taught the people how to plow the fields and plant the seeds. She helped them gather in their harvests. They loved the Kind Earth Mother and gladly obeyed her. They also loved her daughter, the beautiful Persephone.

Persephone wandered all day in the meadows among the flowers. Wherever she went, birds singing merrily flocked after her. The people said, "Where Persephone is, there is the warm sunshine. Flowers bloom when she smiles. Listen to her voice: it is like a bird's song."

Demeter wished always to have her child near her. But one day Persephone went alone into a meadow near the sea. She made a wreath of delicate blossoms for her hair, and gathered all the flowers that her apron could hold.

Far away across the meadow she saw a white flower gleaming. She ran to it and found it was a narcissus, but far more beautiful than any she had ever seen. On a single stem were a hundred blossoms. She tried to pick it, but the stem would not break. With all her strength she grasped it, and slowly the narcissus came up by the roots.

It left a great opening in the earth that grew larger and larger. Soon Persephone heard a rumbling like thunder under her feet. Then she saw four black horses coming toward her from the opening. Behind them was a chariot made of gold and precious stones. In it sat a dark, stern man. It was Hades.

He had come up from his land of darkness, and was shading his eyes with his hands. In the sunny meadow Hades saw Persephone standing, beautiful with flowers. He reached out and caught her in his arms, and placed her in the chariot beside him.

The flowers fell from her apron. "Oh, my lovely flowers!" she cried, "I have lost them all."

Then she saw the stern face of Hades. Frightened, she stretched out her hands to kind Apollo, who was driving his chariot in the sky overhead. She called to her mother, Demeter, for help. No one answered her.

Hades drove straight toward his dark underground home. The horses seemed to fly. As they left the light, Hades tried to comfort Persephone. He told her of the wonders of his kingdom, of all the gold and silver and precious stones which he possessed. In the dim light, as they went along, Persephone saw gems glittering on every side, but she did not care for them, and she wept bitterly.

"I have been very lonely in my vast kingdom," said Hades. "I am bringing you to my palace, where you shall be my queen. You shall share all my riches with me." But Persephone did not want to be a queen. She longed only for her mother and the bright sunshine and the sweet-smelling meadows.

Soon they came to the palace of Hades. It seemed very dark and dismal to Persephone, and very cold, too. A feast was ready for her, but she would not eat. She knew that anyone who ate in Hades' home could never again return to earth. She was very unhappy, though Hades tried in many ways to please her.

Everything and everyone on the earth was unhappy, too. One by one the flowers hung their heads and said, "We cannot bloom, for Persephone has gone."

The trees dropped their leaves and moaned, "Persephone has gone, gone."

The birds flew away, calling, "We cannot sing, for Persephone has gone."

Demeter was more miserable than anyone else. She had heard Persephone call her, and had gone swiftly home to find her. She searched all the earth for her child. She asked everyone she met on her way these questions, "Have you seen Persephone? Where is Persephone?"

The only answer she ever received was, "Gone, gone. Persephone is gone!"

Soon Demeter became a wrinkled old woman. No one would have known that she was the kind mother who had always smiled on the people. She sat mourning day and night, her great tears falling steadily upon the cold ground. Nothing grew upon the earth and all became dreary and barren.

It was useless for the people to plow the soil. It was useless to plant the seeds. Nothing could grow without the help of Demeter, and all the people were idle and sad.

Demeter wandered into many lands, and when she found no one on earth who could tell her about Persephone, she looked up toward the sky. There she saw Apollo in his bright chariot. He was not driving as high in the sky as he was wont to do. He had been hidden by dark mists so that no one had been able to see him for many days.

Demeter knew that he must know about Persephone, for he could see all things on earth and in the sky.

"O great Apollo," she cried, "pity me, and tell me where my child is hidden."

Then Apollo told Demeter that Hades had carried Persephone away and that she was with him in his underground home.

Demeter hastened to great Father Zeus, who could do all things. She asked him to send to Hades for her daughter. Zeus called Hermes. He bade him go as swiftly as the wind to the home of Hades.

Hermes gladly obeyed, and he whispered the joyful news to all he met on his way. "I am going for Persephone. I am going for Persephone. Be ready to welcome her back!"

He soon arrived in the gloomy kingdom under the earth. He gave Hades the message from Zeus, He told about the barren earth and of how Demeter was mourning for her child. He said she would not let anything grow until Persephone came back. "The people will starve if she does not soon return," he said.

Then Persephone wept bitterly, for that very day she had eaten a pomegranate and swallowed six of its seeds, and she remembered that whoever ate in Hades' home could never return to earth again.

But Hades took pity upon her and said, "Go, Persephone, back to the sunshine. But the law must be obeyed, and you shall come back every year to stay with me one month for each seed that you have eaten. That is all I ask."

Joy gave her wings, and as swiftly as Hermes himself, Persephone flew up into the sunshine. Suddenly the flowers sprang up. The birds flocked together and sang;

the trees put on bright green leaves. Everything, great and small, began to say in its own language, "Be happy, for Persephone has come! Persephone has come!"

Demeter was so benumbed with sorrow that she did not at once heed these voices. But soon she saw the great changes all about her and was puzzled. "Can the earth be ungrateful? Does it so soon forget my sweet Persephone?" she cried.

It was not long, however, before her own face grew radiant. She became once more the kind Earth Mother, for she held again her beloved child in her arms. When Demeter found that Persephone could stay with her only half the year, she brought out the choicest treasures from the storehouse, and while Persephone stayed, the world was filled with beauty and joy. When she was gone, Demeter carefully covered the rivers and lakes, and spread a soft white blanket over the sleeping earth.

KEY THOUGHTS

You may be asking yourself how this ancient myth could possibly be relevant to the topic of excuses. Let me ask you this: who or what is your Persephone? Who or what is "making" you wait for the completion of your dreams, desires, and goals? What do you tell yourself about the waiting process and about when you will stop waiting? These are tough questions, especially if the answers have worked for you up until now.

My Persephone was my overly busy schedule of work, caring for my family, and trying to find time for all the other things I thought I wanted to do. I finally realized that Honey, my imaginary friend and built-in excuse from my childhood, had merely returned in grander form. It sounded much better even to myself to blame Persephone instead of Honey!

Honey had eventually "moved away". How could I get Persephone to "move away" as well? The key for me was simply in the recognition that I had traded one excuse for another. I learned to stop making excuses when I was asked to do something I didn't want to do, for example. My new and improved answer was, "No, but thanks for thinking of me." I realized that no one was particularly interested in why I wasn't going to do something they had asked. In fact, they probably stopped listening as soon as they heard "No." That was a very liberating thought.

The next step in the process for me was to recognize when I was making excuses to myself. That was more difficult. My excuses and rationalizations had worked so well for so long that I was unaware of many of them. I enlisted the aid of my mentor at the time to point them out to me. That was the key I needed. Pretty soon I was aware of them myself and worked to eliminate them. I no longer am working with the same mentor, and I may not have eliminated all of my excuses, but I know what to look for and how to rid myself of the ones that are interfering with what I want to accomplish.

Here is a way to you to put these key thoughts into action for yourself.

- Think about how you respond to criticism. Most of us have to deal with some form of criticism on a daily basis, or at least quite frequently. Criticism isn't just a verbal attack. It can be a sarcastic comment, a raised eyebrow signifying mild disapproval, and so on. I don't want to sensitize you to the point where you see or hear criticism in every exchange, but be aware of your response to real or perceived criticism. Do you rationalize your actions or lack of action in a silent response or in what you say back to the other person? When you rationalize in this way, you might as well say, "Honey told me to" or "We're out of mustard." It is about the same thing; as pundits love to say, "Any excuse will do."

  This is a tough one, I know, but for the next few days or a week, analyze your responses. Don't pass judgment on yourself at this point. Just notice what you do and what your thought process is.

- Think about your response when someone asks you to do something you don't necessarily want to do or something you don't have time to do. What is your usual response? Do you say, as I did, "Oh, I can't. I have to *blah...blah...blah.* I'm not good at *blah...blah...blah.* I can't possibly fit *blah...blah...blah...* into my schedule because I have to *blah...blah...blah.*

You get the idea. The same principle applies here. Don't pass judgment on yourself at this point and for heaven's sake don't make an excuse. That's what we're trying to avoid, remember? Just make note of your typical response to an undesirable request.

- Think about your response to compliments and favorable statements made to you or about you. This is the most difficult area for some of us to deal with. Remembering that a simple "thank you" is sufficient, or "that's kind of you" or even "I appreciate your feedback", how do you react? Do you pooh-pooh the whole idea that you could possibly have done something well, that you look attractive, or whatever the statement might be?

Again, just take note of your typical response. This area may seem contrary to the theme of this lesson, but I believe that our response to compliments says as much or more about our self-image and/or public image as our response to criticism. Is this an area in which you could make some positive changes?

CONNECTING TO THE SPIRITUAL

How can you find a spiritual connection in an essay and exercises on excuses? Consider the talents you have been given (that's God-given) and you begin to see the connection. When we allow our preconceived notions about what we "should" do control our actions, it is easy to fall back on excuses and patterns of behavior that may have worked for us in the past. When I looked more closely at what I was doing, I was surprised to discover that my tried and true excuses and patterns weren't really working after all. What's more, I was in a state of denial about the handiwork of God in my life. I realize that's a strong statement, but I needed strong statements and stronger resolve to change my patterns into honest assessments of my talents and abilities.

What a revelation that was! And how liberated I felt. That's my goal for you as well. Reveal yourself to yourself and liberate yourself from whatever has been holding you back. As you work to incorporate these ideas into your self-image, allow plenty of time to reflect, to be in meditation or prayer, and to record your thoughts in your journal or exercise book.

Keys to getting started with this idea:

- Review the material that you have already written in response to exercises you addressed earlier in this essay or in others.
- Identify any patterns that you see emerging. Is your awareness of your potential heightened by these challenges to preconceived notions?

Prayer Suggestions

- Pray for the insight to see your full potential.

- Pray with gratitude for the God given talents that you are already expressing.

- Pray with hope for the God given talents that you are ready to discover.

- Pray for the ability to react positively to criticism.

- Pray for the ability to react positively to praise and compliments.

- Pray for the ability and/or skill to exchange any excuse you might make for a useful and productive alternative.

PERSONAL MEDITATION

As you reflect on what you are reading and on what you have written, you are engaging in a powerful form of personal meditation. Additional thoughts may flow to you as you open your mind to spirit-filled energy. Take note of these thoughts and random ideas that flow in and out of your consciousness. There is a power there that you can use.

I believe that we are endowed with a spiritual element. I also believe that our various forms of religious practices are our attempt to respond to that spiritual element placed within us. If we deny the power within us to make a difference, to effect change, to create harmony, and to eliminate our excuses then we are essentially denying ourselves and our God-given blessings.

SERVING OTHERS
How to Be Available

1. With a friend, or on your own, list some of the excuses you are apt to make in a given situation. For each one, list the advantages of the excuse itself. There are some, or you wouldn't use it. Next, list any disadvantages there might be. This can be much more difficult, because until now you have relied on the excuse to protect yourself in some way.

2. Tackle one of the excuses from your first list. List some disadvantages of not using that excuse any more. Next, list some advantages of not using it. Again, this will be the more difficult.

3. This next part is important and will lead to lasting changes in your reactions to situations you face. For each situation that in the past has led to the use of one of your excuses, work to develop a statement that buys you time to consider it. For example, instead of saying "No, I don't have time to do that for you," try saying something like "That depends; tell me more about it".

PUTTING IT ALL TOGETHER

You may be wondering how the exercises mentioned in this chapter will help you to eliminate excuses from your own life and how you can assist others in this part of the journey to a surrendered life. I believe that you can be a model, not of perfection, but of one person's attempt to improve herself. You can also, in a loving way, encourage others to eliminate excuses from their lives. What an opportunity for you to work with someone else as an accountability buddy, a confidante, a person in a trusting relationship that is based on telling each other the truth.

Some of the exercises may not have seemed relevant to you when you read through this material the first time. That is understandable. You may want to consider revisiting the exercises and your earlier responses periodically. You may be surprised at what you find. Perhaps your perspective has changed. That is growth and that is what this lifelong journey is about.

Enjoy the process, painful as it can be at times. At the beginning of this chapter, I described excuses as "our friends", ever willing to bail us out of situations that we are not ready to face. I hope you have found new "friends" as a result of the work you have done in this chapter. Take stock of the changes you have made and reward yourself in a positive manner. Keep on the path to your surrendered life and relish each moment of revelation, relationship, and reward.

Chapter Fourteen

Claim Your Abundance

PERSONAL REFLECTION

Do you remember when you realized that you lived a life of abundance? Neither do I, but I believe that it began to occur to me sometime during my Kindergarten or first grade year. I noticed that some of the other children in my class were sad, scared, and/ or hungry. I could not have explained it then in those terms, but I began to understand "the haves and have-nots" so to speak.

I grew up on a self-sustaining farm in southwest Washington State. My parents were both educated and had good jobs before I was born. My father was a research chemist for a paper mill and my mother was a school secretary. At the beginning of World War II, my father left the paper mill to go farming. Farming was considered part of the war effort and he could have gotten his job back after the war. He didn't want it. He did go back and film safety movies for the paper mill school and occasionally provided tractor work for the mill property, but he no longer worked full time. Neither did my mother, who had left the school district at the end of the 1942 school year. I was born in 1945 and by then my parents were fully involved in the farm life and its activities.

The income derived from the various crops was sufficient to raise a family, educate its children, and provide an abundant life. Our farm produced chickens, eggs, berries of all kinds, apples, peaches, filberts, walnuts, beef, pork, milk, cream, butter, and mounds of vegetables. At one time, for a period of about ten years, my dad hired 500 young people every year to pick the various crops, especially pole green beans. Our farm not only was very productive, it served as a major employer for the teens and young adults in our community.

Did I appreciate all of that? No, I didn't. I wanted to be like the little girls in town who had roller skates and the sidewalks to skate on. Of course I knew that they all wanted to live in the country and have a horse to ride and have kittens in the barn to play with, but that didn't matter to my childish mind. I can still hear my father proudly stating, "Our family has everything except money". Why did I miss the message? I understand it now.

LOOKING INWARD

This simple story has lessons for all of us in my opinion. There have been other times in my life during which I have not fully appreciated and explored the abundance that is all around me. Friends, family, and other relationships provide an abundance of learning opportunities, experiences, and blessings that can truly abound in the treasures that reward us on a daily basis. The attitude of gratitude is one that I continue to work on. For a long time I have had the statement "act on my good intentions" written across the top of my weekly planner. I'm improving in this area, but I still don't always express my appreciation to my friends for blessing me with their friendship. I believe that these two concepts, the abundant life and gratitude for the abundance, are two sides of the same great idea.

As I continue to mature in my understanding of the nature of our relationship to our creator and each other, I am more fully aware of the implications of the statement," To whom much is given, much is expected." How can we "give as much as is expected?" We have to recognize at some level that giving is a privilege. There are many ways in which we can give of ourselves out of our abundance. Without even considering financial giving, there are many ways in which we can share from our abundance. The church I attend has a litany that states that we will give our prayers, our presence, our gifts, and our service. No matter what faith each of us practices, there are similar statements of faith in action. Faith in action is a good way to apply the abundance we feel and is, I believe, a natural outcome of our desire to give back in some form.

WISDOM FROM THE AGES

The two concepts I mentioned earlier provide the fiber of many of the folktales that I loved as a child. A perceived lack of abundance and gratitude for the abundance when it reappears are central themes in many favorite stories. Here is one of them.

The Tiny Little Cottage

There once was an old man who lived with his old wife in a tiny little cottage in a tiny little village. The old man grew discontented with the size of his tiny cottage and went to ask the wisest man of the village what he should do. The wise man told him to bring the cat into the house. The cat normally lived in the barn with the cow, the chickens, the donkey, the pig, and the geese. The old man couldn't see how this would help the cottage be larger, but he did as the wise man suggested.

After a few days of pushing the cat out of places it wasn't supposed to be and crushing its tail under the rocking chair, the old man went back to the wise man and complained about the seemingly even smaller house. The wise man told him to bring in the dog. The dog normally lived under the porch. Again, the old man could not understand the reasoning of the wise man, but he did as he was told.

After a few more days of trying to live with both the cat and the dog underfoot all the time and listening to the growling and the hissing, the old man stormed back to the wise man and argued bitterly that the solutions were absolutely not working.

The wise man told the old man to bring in the cow and the chickens. When the old man did as the wise man suggested, all the animals made a huge mess in the cottage and angered the old woman. The old couple agreed, however, that the wise man had their best interests in mind so they decided to continue following his advice. After a few more days, all the animals were living in the house making noises of all kinds, smells of all kinds, and chaos of all kinds.

The old man finally had enough and took matters into his own hands. One by one he put the animals back where they belonged. Then he and his wife cleaned and scrubbed the cottage until every surface gleamed. That night the old man and the old woman agreed that, indeed, the cottage was much larger now than it had been before they had asked for help from the wise man.

KEY THOUGHTS

We learn pretty much in the same way that the old couple learned their lesson. Abundance and gratitude are relative terms. We bring our upbringing, our habits, our life experiences, and the influences of our environment to every new situation. The feeling of abundance and the attitude of gratitude are developmental and incremental skills that can be acquired, in my opinion. No doubt you are familiar with the ancient proverbs that suggest man is not content if he falls even a little short of his expectations; he is supremely content if he exceeds his expectations by even a little bit.

Let's take another look at expectations. We have our own, of course, but the world has expectations for us as well. I believe we are happiest when we expect the best from ourselves and hope for the best from our world.

I can hear you now. "You haven't met my boss! You don't understand the pressures on my time. People have unreasonable expectations for me, for my children and spouse, for my ....." That's all true. I haven't met your boss, I don't know what pressures you feel, and

I certainly don't understand what sorts of expectations are being placed on you. However, we all pretty much have the same issues in our lives. Whether the big issue for you is health, financial concerns, relationships, emotional issues, time, or balance, you are still "you".

Remember "count your blessings"? It's difficult to see the good in a difficult or dangerous situation. There may be something good in a different part of your life that will sustain you while you are struggling in one area. Work to recognize the good, talk about it, and use it to develop an attitude of strength and gratitude that will encourage you to continue your struggle with optimism.

CONNECTING TO THE SPIRITUAL

Finding a spiritual connection between the concepts of abundance, an attitude of gratitude and your current reality may be a challenge. Let me share some well-known examples from an email "pass along" that may serve to emphasize the abundance of your current reality, no matter how bleak it may appear at times. These examples are in no way meant to make any of us feel guilty about wishing things were better for us. It is human nature to desire improvement in all areas of our lives. Only people without hope have lost the desire to better themselves in my opinion.

- If you woke up this morning with more health than illness, you are more blessed than the million who will not survive the week.
- If you have never experienced the danger of battle, the loneliness of imprisonment, the agony of torture, or the pangs of starvation, you are ahead of 500 million people in the world.
- If you have food in the refrigerator, clothes on your back, a roof over your head, and a place to sleep, you are richer than 75% of the world.
- If you have money in the bank and spare change in a dish somewhere, you are among the top 8% of the world's wealthy.
- If you can read this message, you are more blessed than over two billion people in the world who cannot read at all.

Those are astonishing statistics. How can we use these comparisons to connect to the spirit-filled existence that we want for ourselves, our families, our friends, our communities, and the world? Awareness is the first step in change. If we raise our awareness of issues like the ones mentioned above, our subconscious will go to work to find solutions if we direct it to do so. An effective means of directing our subconscious is the following four-step process.

1. Clear your mind of everyday distractions. Some people find music helpful; others find it an additional distraction. You will need to discover what works for you.

2. Reflect on a particular issue that was successful for you in the past. Were you able to resolve a conflict, lose weight, make or maintain a friendship? Whatever it was, think about the ways in which you accomplished it and the way you felt. Written affirmations of your success will further guide you.

3. Bring as much of that feeling as you can as you begin to focus on a new, perhaps problematic, situation. If you begin to feel anxious or frustrated, retreat to the second step of this process or leave it until next time. Continue to approach the new situation whenever you have regained the relaxed, happy feeling you experienced in step two.

4. Reflect on the ideas that flow to you when you think about the new situation. Record your ideas, even ones that don't seem to relate. You may find a kernel of value that can be developed.

Prayer Suggestions

- Pray in thanksgiving for the ability to clear your mind of everyday distractions.

- Pray in anticipation of an increased awareness of the abundance you already experience.

- Pray in anticipation of an increasingly grateful attitude for all that you are.

- Pray for strength and courage to deal with change.

- Pray for wisdom.

- Pray for opportunities to express your gratitude for your abundance in ways that will make a difference to someone else.

PERSONAL MEDITATION

Opening your mind to your possibilities is one of the most spiritual activities in which we can engage. Energy from the entire universe is said to flow through us. If we can train our minds to be aware of it, receptive to it, and courageous enough to apply it, just consider the possibilities.

Many books discuss the readiness with which the world steps aside so that those with purpose and vision might pass, even coming to their aid in carrying out their aims. Much of the wisdom literature of the ages focuses on similar principles. How can we deny the existence of such a force? We can all develop an intuitive sense of being present, being receptive, being ready to step out in our own personal faith journey.

SERVING OTHERS
How to Be Available

With so much on our own plates, in terms of growing into this new awareness, how do we manage to serve others at the same time? Consider the concept of the leader as servant. This age old idea is re-emerging as a powerful tool in business, in interpersonal relationships, and in the ways we set goals. Serving others does not mean that we should abandon our own needs and the fulfillment of them by ourselves or by anyone else.

How often has someone come to you with a problem or a complaint? More times than you can count is the logical answer. Does that person really want you to suggest a solution or to fix the problem for them? Probably not. In many situations like this, the other person simply wants a sympathetic (or at least patient) ear. Being heard is underrated. Being heard and understood is very underrated. You can provide a wonderful service to others by learning to be a nonjudgmental listener, one who can be trusted to hold a confidence.

If you're not sure of your role in a situation like this, ask the other person what they would like you to do with the information. Sometimes you'll be asked to act on it, but more often you'll simply be thanked for listening.

Gaining the appreciation of another adds to your feeling of abundance and increases your attitude of gratitude. Try it. Be proud of what you can do for someone else in the simple act of being available to them.

PUTTING IT ALL TOGETHER

Apply what you've learned from the different sections of this chapter to your everyday experience. Record your responses to the thoughts that are triggered by reminders or new ideas. Set a goal for the number of times you will notice that you are experiencing a feeling of gratitude. Record what makes you feel this way. Make a point of assessing your current areas of abundance and set a goal for an increase in your sense of well-being. You can conquer any feelings of inferiority or disappointment by learning to focus on the good that may come as a result of difficulty. Becoming a stronger, more spirit filled person is an example that you may find encouraging.

Above all, believe that an abundant life is yours. Work for balance. Strive to take care of yourself. Pray, reflect, and meditate every day. Keep track of your journey in some way. Continue to look back on your past experiences for what they can teach you. Look forward in anticipation that the best is yet to come.

Chapter Fifteen

Make Your Friendships Count

PERSONAL REFLECTION

When I think back over my lifetime and consider all the wonderful friends and acquaintances that have blessed me and helped me create the person I am, I am struck by a novel thought. Not many of those friendships have been collaborative in the sense that they have been a relationship of equals. In many cases, my friend or acquaintance took the lead, making decisions about what we would do, where we would go, and even (especially around the 7th grade) deciding what we would wear. In many cases, I took the lead. Only a few were balanced in the decision making process. It's those friendships I treasure most.

Those equal relationships, which were mutually beneficial in the personal development and maturity of both of us, have taught me some valuable lessons about working collaboratively as an adult. I believe that collaboration is an elusive element in many of our relationships, even in our relationship with our spouse or other family members.

I watched my parents set the example for positive collaboration with what looked like ease and continual agreement. Little did I know! I learned much later that they were wise enough to disagree in private and to present a united front. I never got away with the standard trick of saying, "Mom said it's OK with her, if it's OK with you, Dad." Dad always checked with Mom to see if that's how it really was. Naturally, it worked the other way, too. As I grew older, I realized that when it came to matters affecting the whole family my dad was the voice for the family.

My mom's role was as sounding board, decision partner, and support. Interestingly, my dad's role was as sounding board, decision partner, and support also. Another component of this kind of collaborative friendship or relationship is that each person must bring his or her own unique and essential "spiritual" self to the table. Each of the components of their roles taught me valuable lessons that I've applied to the best of my ability as I've worked to form collaborative relationships and friendships as an adult.

LOOKING INWARD

I believe that the role of sounding board is a proactive one. Passive listening is not the same as active listening. Active listening has elements of affirmation, clarification, focus, and even correction imbedded in it. As an active listener, it is our job to affirm what the speaker has done well in his or her attempt to communicate with us. It is our responsibility to be sure that we understand what the speaker is saying. Ask questions if a point is not clear in such a way that the speaker is not put on the defensive. Identify points of agreement, points of disagreement to be worked out, points that need clarification, or any other areas that need to be revisited. Write down what you need to in order to begin the next conversation or conference effectively. Is every conversation this formal? Of course not, but important matters needing decisions of consequence will benefit from these steps. Open, honest communication is the essence of successfully being each other's sounding board.

As authors, we have found this role to be relatively easy for each of us. We have so much respect for one another that actively listening, affirming, clarifying, staying focused, and offering correction has developed new depth and strength to our partnership. In fact, we may actually play this role better in our relationship with each other than either of us does with our husbands!

The role of decision partner is a vital one. The key to effective decision-making in a collaborative relationship is effective communication. If the role of sounding board has been played successfully, the role of decision partner is an easier task. I believe the basic element of decision-making is preparation. Lack of preparation leads to much second-guessing and does nothing to instill confidence in each other. This is not to say that any of us should close our minds to additional information that may alter or cancel the original decision. Indeed, open-mindedness is key to most functions of most relationships. However, when the time is right to move forward, making a decision and acting upon it are the only ways anything is ever accomplished.

As we worked together on this book, we each took on the responsibility of making key decisions based upon lots of conversation, coffee, and commitment. Most of the decisions we make when we collaborate in any process are jointly made with input, suggestions, compromise, and eventual agreement from every person involved.

The role of support is often underestimated. How often have you witnessed or participated in what was supposedly a collaborative process and discovered to your dismay that once decisions had been reached there was an ominous undercurrent of dissatisfaction? This is not fair and has no place in any relationship. It seems to me that given the opportunity to participate in the process we must express all reservations, be convinced that the agreed upon decisions are in the best interest of all parties, and be ready to wholeheartedly support the results.

In spite of what I said in the previous paragraph, I realize that sometimes, perhaps especially in a work environment, not everything is as it appears. I remember feeling betrayed by administrative decisions in which I was led to believe that my point of view counted when, in reality, decisions had been reached before I was even asked to participate. Has this ever happened to you? Has it ever not happened? What made the difference? I confess that at times I went along to get along. Have you had this experience as well?

What can we do to prevent such feelings of frustration and outrage on the part of the people we need to work with? I think part of the answer can be found in the implementation of each of the three roles I have already described.

WISDOM FROM THE AGES

None of us is as smart as all of us. That seems to be a central theme in hundreds of children's stories, folk tales, and homespun stories from around the world. The idea of cooperation and collaboration to solve problems is an ancient concept that is still fresh today. Many cultures have shared the following story that illustrates the concept of working collaboratively to solve a common problem.

The Enormous Turnip

There was once an old man who lived with his wife in a small cottage on the edge of the village. The old man was a wonderful gardener and many people from the village would ask him for advice about gardening. He enjoyed telling the villagers about his vegetables, especially his prize turnips. He became rather vain about his skills and began to believe that only he had the proper touch in the raising of crops.

One fall day he was tending his garden and getting ready to harvest the vegetables. As he neared the end of the last row of turnips, he came to one that he could not pull out by the leaves as he was usually able to do. Reluctantly, he called to his wife to come and help him. "Good wife," he said, "I find that I am unable to pull out this enormous turnip. I need your help."

His wife was pleased that he asked since he had grown ever more possessive of his garden and too proud for his own good in her opinion. She put her arms around his middle and pulled as hard as she could while he was pulling on the leaves of the enormous turnip. Even together they could not budge it.

The old man walked to his son's house and invited the grandson and granddaughter to come and help. Even the four of them could not dislodge the turnip from the ground. They added the dog and the cat, and they all pulled. Finally, a bird that was flying by saw what they were doing.

The bird pulled on the cat. The cat pulled on the dog. The dog pulled on the granddaughter. The granddaughter pulled on the grandson. The grandson pulled on the old woman. The old woman pulled on the old man and out popped the enormous turnip. Of course, the bird took full credit for solving the problem.

For the rest of his life the old man was eager to allow people to help him tend his garden. He gladly helped his neighbors and gladly received their help in all the ways that good neighbors work together.

KEY THOUGHTS

Perhaps you are aware of people who have lost their employment because, while productive, they are not recognized as team players. Competition rather than collaboration seems to cause envy, jealousy, and all kinds of turf wars within corporate America, within churches and other civic organizations, and even at home.

We are aware of women who started out as good friends to take on a project to improve their schools, create safer neighborhood parks, increase the percentage of voter registrations, and so on. Over the course of the project, they became alienated, angry and frustrated with delay, annoyed by seemingly insignificant style differences and so on and ended the project no longer speaking to one another.

I believe that truly inspired relationships, the ones that really count, are based on a willingness to empower the other person. How is that done? One key element of empowerment is a person's ability to delegate. Delegation is defined as "the process of transferring the responsibility for a specific task to another person and empowering that individual to accomplish the task effectively." Planning a class reunion, a neighborhood block party, or even assigning household tasks fall into the category of delegation. Projects at work lend themselves to delegation as well.

I have experienced many such projects in which the group leader was not willing to empower anyone on the team. Those projects often failed because of infighting, turf wars, and other equally destructive territorial disputes. How sad. On the other hand, I have experienced projects that soared beyond our most optimistic expectations due to everyone's willingness to take on his or her individual tasks, empower others to succeed and share the results.

Another key strategy that will empower another person is one my parents demonstrated so well. That is, disagree in private and present a united front. In a business setting, in situations at home, or in committee work of all kinds, disagreeing with someone or correcting someone is best done in private. Praise and compliments are wonderful to hear, especially if others overhear them.

The most significant ingredient in collaboration is what I term synergistic energy. Synergism is defined as a process in which the sum is greater than the parts. This is not mathematical, certainly, but true when it comes to the dynamics of human relationships. The energy you experience when you are of kindred minds is an awesome, spirit-inspired force that mows down obstacles. Andrew Carnegie called it the mastermind principle. He gathered around himself such eminent business leaders as Charles Schwab, Henry Ford and others. Even though their business interests were different, they served each other as sounding boards, decision partners, and support. Together they accomplished much more than any of them could have done individually.

We can benefit from the same principle when we collaborate, when we empower others, and when we are responsive to our own spirit-endowed abilities. We can make our friendships count.

CONNECTING TO THE SPIRITUAL

One of the most challenging aspects for me in the collaborative process was learning to be responsive to my own spirit-endowed abilities. I believe I can explain my difficulty better by focusing on the concepts of pride and being proud. In my experience, pride, when it takes the form of arrogance or egotism, is a negative force that calls inappropriate attention to ourselves and diminishes our relationships with other people. Being proud of yourself for a challenge met, a task completed, or a shared experience that benefited everyone around you is a positive force that develops both individuals and groups. Once I understood the difference and was able to apply my new awareness to my circumstances, I felt much more connected to the spirit within me that called me to do my best.

This was a huge, life-changing breakthrough for me. I felt empowered for the first time to be who I was called to be. That is, I recognized that I was a child of God who was worthy of whatever success I could achieve. I recognized that my feelings of accomplishment were meant to generate a desire to help other people enjoy the same satisfaction. I recognized that in order to participate fully in the relationships I had with other people and indeed the relationship I had with myself I must be ready to give and to receive in a collaborative sense.

I recognize now that I not only can serve as a leader but I can also create and nurture leadership skills in other people. I have been forever grateful for that insight. It has made all the difference in the way I relate to everyone around me.

Prayer Suggestions

- Pray in gratitude for those whose friendship has encouraged you.

- Pray for the ability to empower others.

- Pray for the ability to be empowered by others.

- Pray for the peace that comes with the understanding that you are worthy to receive the success you have achieved.

- Pray for open, honest communication.

- Pray for the blessing of equal relationships.

PERSONAL MEDITATION

Personal meditation is a powerful habit that can literally change your perception of the way the world works and the ways in which you can relate to your circumstances. I used visualization, prayer, and focused thought to generate an appreciation of collaborative relationships. Even though I had grown up in a home that valued collaboration and cooperation, as I mentioned earlier, I still struggled with the release of control that I perceived was key to working together.

Finally, I came to realize that what I had thought was a release of control was really just allowing another person to empower me. There was no need for me to feel threatened by the process. In fact, I was enriched by the shared experience. I did proceed with caution into this new area. At times I felt the need to pull back when I sensed that the other person was not ready to share on an equal basis. All of these trials (and errors) served to strengthen my skills in teamwork, team building, and team process. I now am able to bring all that I have learned to each new situation. Even situations that I would never have dreamed would lend themselves to collaboration have proved to be more easily conquered because people are willing to take a chance and see if it would work.

I believe that synergistic energy is just waiting for us to receive it. When we are willing to listen to ourselves and direct our subconscious minds to do so, we can move mountains.

SERVING OTHERS
How to Be Available

Collaboration is a perfect example of serving others and being served by others. Think of the amazing projects that various civic groups and churches engage in to serve the community. I believe that none of them would be possible without the synergistic energy that is generated when people collaborate. Food banks, shelters, safety campaigns, animal shelters and pet adoption groups, drives to provide school supplies to needy children, eye glasses drives and so on and so on are some of the myriad examples of the good that is being done all around us. Most of these worthy causes were the idea of one or two people or a small group who believed that the community could be served by their commitment to work together.

You have the power to do that too. It takes an idea, a willingness to risk temporary setbacks, the ability to form and work with teams of people, and a cooperative spirit.

Ask yourself two questions. "Why not?" and "Who's going to stop me?"

PUTTING IT ALL TOGETHER

That's it. Making your friendships count is a matter of believing in yourself, believing in other people, and acting on your good intentions.

- Open your mind to the constant stream of thoughts that flood your every waking moment. Capture the ones that are positive.

- Learn to listen from a deeper level.

- Be courageous about expressing yourself.

- Participate in decision-making.

- Be supportive when you believe in what is being expressed.

- Be ready to offer suggestions.

- Delegate whatever you can. Remember that when you release control you are allowing another person to empower you.

- Track your progress through these tasks as you learn to surrender.

- Affirm your greatness.

- Empower yourself to choose.

However you choose to develop yourself as a collaborative friend, enjoy the process and continue the journey of your spirit filled life.

Notes

Chapter One

Adapted by Susan Reed from original sources and from Caitlin Matthews's retelling. Sandye Brown further adapted this version by substituting "The Black Knight" in place of the name Gromer Somer Joure.

Chapter Two

Hercules Chooses His Path. Adapted by Sandye Brown from "The Labors of Hercules" from *The Treasure Chest of My Bookhouse*, by Olive Beaupre Miller (Chicago: The Bookhouse for Children, 1928).

The Electric Fence Syndrome. Based on "Electric Fence Syndrome" from *Speaker's Sourcebook II*, by Glenn Van Ekeren (New Jersey: Prentice Hall Press, 1994)

Rumi Poem.
http://www.kathrynpetro.com/mindfullife/archives/000389.html. From *Rumi: Fountain of Fire, A Celebration of Life and Love*, courtesy of CalEarth Press, 1994, translated from the Persian by Nader Khalili.

A Sioux Story.
http://www.essentia.com/book/stories/hiddenreality.htm

Chapter Three

A Man in Search of His Luck.
http://www.tellingtales.com/Stories/Stories-Frame.htm

Chaplain John E. Batterson *How to Listen to God.* Pamphlet

See Lee Coit, *Listening: How to Increase Awareness of Your Inner Guide.* San Clemente: Las Brisas Publishing. 1996

See Genie Z. Laborde, *Influencing Integrity: Management Skills for Communication and Negotiation.* Redwood City: Syntony Publishing, 1997.

See **Sally** Cook Parsons, *Learning To Listen With The 'Spiritual Heart',* Special Correspondent to Trinity News. http://www. trinitywallstreet.org/news/article_64.shtml

See Penney Peirce, *The Intuitive Way: A Guide to Living from Inner Wisdom.* Hillsboro: Beyond Words Publishing, Inc., 1997.

See Hal and Sidra Stone, *Embracing Your Inner Critic: Turning Self-Criticism into a Creative Asset.* San Francisco: Harper Collins, 1993.

See Hal and Sidra Stone, *Embracing Ourselves: The Voice Dialogue Manual.* Novato: Nataraj Publishing, 1989.

See Eckhart Tolle, *The Power of Now: A Guide to Spiritual Enlightenment.* Novato: New World Library, 1999

Chapter Four

The Story of the Sage of Herat. http://www.zensufi.com/heart.htm

See Thomas Keating, *Open Mind, Open Heart: The Contemplative Dimension of the Gospel.* New York: Continuum Publishing Company, 1998.

Chapter Five

The Story Of The Sleepy Man. http://www.zensufi.com/sleepy.htm

See Joseph Campbell, *The Power of Myth.* New York: Anchor Publishing, 1991

Chapter Six

The Maiden, the Mountain, and the Serpent. I think my grandfather, Alexander C. Roberts, made this story up. It's been part of our extended family vernacular for over a hundred years and I can't find it anywhere on the Internet. Alexis Mason

Chapter Seven

The Myth of Sisyphus, Albert Camus. Retold by Alexis Mason, according to my philosophy instructor as an undergrad at the University of Puget Sound in 1963

Chapter Eight

The Donkey in the Well. An email "Pass Along".

See Lynn Grabhorn, *Excuse Me, Your Life is Waiting: The Astonishing Power of Feelings.* Charlottesville: Hampton Roads Publishing Company, Inc. 2000

See Dr. Joseph Murphy, *The Power of Your Subconscious Mind.* New York: Bantam Books. 2000

See Catherine Ponder, *The Dynamic Laws of Prosperity: Forces that Bring Riches to You.* Englewood Cliffs: Prentice Hall, Inc. 1976

Chapter Nine:

The Builder. http://www.inspirationalstories.com/1/197.html

Chapter Ten

The Emperor and the Bride. http://www.unveiling.org/Articles/emperor.htm

Chapter Eleven

Hebrews, Chapter 11 from the Revised Standard Version of the Bible.

James, Chapter 2 from the Revised Standard Version of the Bible.

Chapter Twelve

The phrase "pay it forward" comes from the movie *Pay it Forward*. Released in October 2000, directed by Mimi Leder, and starring Kevin Spacey, Helen Hunt and Haley Joel Osment

Luke, chapter 6, verse 38, from the Revised Standard Version of the Bible.

Chapter Thirteen

The Wind and the Sun. Aesop's fable as retold by Alexis Mason

Chapter Fourteen

Persephone. An ancient legend retold by Flora Cooke 1971 edition Childcraft <u>Stories and Fable</u>.

Want More Information?

Companion Activities and other related materials are available for study groups. These materials are designed to support you as you establish a foundation for change, personal development, and empowerment.

One purpose is to provide Blueprint for Spirit-Filled Living workshops for up to fifty people in your church or community setting. We have found that when groups of individuals relate to one another in these settings, they are more effective in applying the skills that are taught as well as enjoying greater satisfaction in life.

We also offer the opportunity for experienced trainers to acquire a license to sell and facilitate Blueprint for Spirit-Filled Living workshops. We are always looking for good people interested in leading workshops. For more information on training opportunities or to schedule a Blueprint for Spirit-Filled Living workshop in your area, visit us at www.InspiredConnections.com.

About the Authors

Sandye Brown spent more than 20 years in corporate management before establishing Wide Awake, Inc., a company specializing in organizational and leadership transformation. Since 1992 she has worked as an executive coach to Fortune 500 companies including Sears, Allstate, and GE Capital. As a transformational consultant, Sandye helps organizations develop collaborative and compassionate work environments. Sandye earned a Bachelors degree from York College in Economics and Psychology. She is also a graduate of the Professional Coaching Certification Program, and is a certified practitioner of Neuro Linguistic Programming. Having overcome many personal challenges as a result of her own spiritual transformation, Sandye also works with women executives to help them more consciously integrate their own unique form of spirituality into their lives. She and her husband, Ben, live in Vancouver, Washington.

Alexis Mason is a master educator with a passion for lifelong learning and nurturing learning in others. She holds a Masters degree in Education from Portland State University and has accumulated more than 30 years of experience teaching for the State of Washington public school system and for City University. A successful business owner and trainer, Alexis loves helping others achieve success in their lives

Alexis and her husband, Dave, live outside Camas, Washington on the farm that was her childhood home. Alexis states that living close to the land inspires her and raises her awareness of stewardship, two concepts that are relevant to the blueprint for spirit filled living.

In addition to their work together as authors, Sandye and Alexis are partners in *Inspired Connections*, where they develop and deliver workshops and other programs to help women grow in self-understanding, self-love, and learning as they affirm and expand their faith, their self-awareness, and their service to their families and communities, and the organizations in which they are involved.